# Literature-Based Reading Activities

## FIFTH EDITION

**Ruth Helen Yopp**

*California State University, Fullerton*

**Hallie Kay Yopp**

*California State University, Fullerton*

**ALLYN & BACON**

Boston   New York   San Francisco
Mexico City   Montreal   Toronto   London   Madrid   Munich   Paris
Hong Kong   Singapore   Tokyo   Cape Town   Sydney

**Executive Editor:** Aurora Martínez Ramos
**Series Editorial Assistant:** Jacqueline Gillen
**Executive Marketing Manager:** Krista Clark
**Production Editor:** Annette Joseph
**Editorial Production Service:** Lynda Griffiths
**Composition Buyer:** Linda Cox
**Manufacturing Buyer:** Megan Cochran
**Electronic Composition:** Denise Hoffman
**Interior Design:** Denise Hoffman
**Cover Designer:** Elena Sidorova

For related titles and support materials, visit our online catalog at
www.pearsonhighered.com.

Between the time website information is gathered and then published, it is not unusual
for some sites to have closed. Also, the transcription of URLs can result in typographical
errors. The publisher would appreciate notification where these errors occur so that they
may be corrected in subsequent editions.

ISBN-10: 0-13-714425-3
ISBN-13: 978-0-13-714425-9

Printed in the United States of America
10  9  8  7  6  5  4  3  2      B-R    13  12  11  10  09

**Allyn & Bacon**
**is an imprint of**

www.pearsonhighered.com

ISBN-10: 0-13-714425-3
ISBN-13: 978-0-13-714425-9

# Contents

# Preface

Literature can be a powerful force in the lives of human beings. It can make us feel, think, and wonder. It can provide us with exciting, interesting information and new ways of looking at the world. It can change who we are forever.

*Literature-Based Reading Activities* is based on the beliefs that quality literature is an essential component of classroom activity and learning and that teachers should engage their students in thinking deeply about ideas in literature, making connections with literature, and responding to literature in ways that enrich their lives. It is also based on the beliefs that students bring unique perspectives, experiences, and contexts to their reading of literature and that social interaction is at the heart of learning. Thus, in this book we share activities that are intended to inspire and support students as they engage with ideas in books; to bring themselves to the literature; and to expand their understandings, perspectives, and responses through interactions with others.

The organization of this fifth edition remains the same as previous editions. Chapter One provides important background information. Chapters Two, Three, and Four provide descriptions of pre-, during, and postreading activities for literature-based reading experiences, along with examples of their application at several grade levels. Examples are shared for a variety of genres, including folktales, fantasy, realistic fiction, historical fiction, poetry, biographies, and informational books. Chapter Five focuses on writing and publishing student work in response to reading. A few important final comments are offered in the Afterword, and lists of exciting websites that have the potential to enrich the literature experience are provided in the Appendix.

New to this edition are the following:

- More explicit attention to writing and its role in a rich literature program

**English learners**

- New activities that more directly focus on writing in response to literature

- English learners icon highlights tips for the teacher looking for assistance in giving literature-based reading activities to English learners

- A discussion of differentiation and suggestions for differentiation throughout the book

**Technology**

- A discussion of new literacies and how technology, including the Internet, can expand students' responses to literature in powerful ways

- New activities that make use of technology

- Twelve new activities and many new examples from recent award-winning literature

We wish to acknowledge the following reviewers who provided helpful comments about the book: Albertaeve S. Abington-Pitre (University of Louisiana at Lafayette), Beverly J. Boulware (The University of Texas at Arlington), Paula Boxie (Miami University, Oxford), Patricia Hewett (University of Tennessee, Martin), and Dixie Kelly (Sam Houston State University).

We are also grateful to the following people for their contributions to this book: Nancy Brewbaker, Paula Gray, and Alan Saldivar, Example 3.26; Doreen Fernandez, Janie Frigge, Kimberly Hennessy, and Thursa Williams, Example 4.4; and Jeanine Rossi, retelling picture book example. We thank our colleague Tim Green for reviewing our technology additions.

We extend a special thanks to Aurora Martinez, our editor at Allyn and Bacon, for her valuable insights and important contributions to our thinking. We also thank Lynda Griffiths for her role in the production of this book.

Finally, many thanks go to our supportive husbands, Tom Edwards and Bert Slowik, for all the things they do that make it possible for us to write, and to our children, Bill, Dan, Peter, and Erica, who remind us daily of the importance of sharing great books with children.

### CHAPTER ONE

# Using Literature in the Classroom

## Literature in the Classroom

Literature plays an important role in the lives and learning of students in many classrooms. In these classrooms, teachers read aloud good stories and interesting informational books, they provide regular independent reading time along with rich classroom libraries, they structure opportunities for students to share their responses to books with one another, and they explore works of literature with their students as part of the instructional program. Some teachers implement a literature-based reading program in which high-quality literature serves as the basis of reading instruction, and others supplement published reading programs with works of literature or integrate literature into other areas of the curriculum. The fortunate students of all these teachers benefit in many ways from the literature-rich experiences and environments their teachers provide; chief among these is that they experience the joy and satisfaction of reading.

Kiefer, Hepler, and Hickman (2006) stated that the intrinsic value of literature alone should be sufficient to give it a place in the curriculum. However, there is considerable evidence that it contributes to literacy development as well. Literature, for example, facilitates language development in both younger and older students (Chomsky, 1972; Morrow, 1992; Nagy, Herman, & Anderson, 1985). It promotes reading achievement (Cohen, 1968; DeFord, 1981; Feitelson, Kita, & Goldstein, 1986; Galda & Cullinan, 2003; Morrow, 1992). It positively influences students' perceptions of and attitudes toward reading (Eldredge & Butterfield, 1986; Hagerty, Hiebert, & Owens, 1989; Larrick, 1987; Morrow, 1992, 2003; Morrow, O'Connor, & Smith, 1990; Tunnell & Jacobs, 1989). It also influences writing ability (DeFord, 1981, 1984; Eckhoff, 1983; Lancia, 1997) and deepens knowledge of written language and written linguistic features (Purcell-Gates, McIntyre, & Freppon, 1995). Further, it has been suggested that the use of literature in the content areas (such as social studies and science) results in greater student understanding of and engagement with the content (Bean, 2000; Morrow & Gambrell, 2000; Saul, 2004).

When we examine what we believe are the goals of literacy instruction—to develop students' ability to learn with text; to expand their ability to think broadly, deeply, and critically about ideas in text; to promote personal responses to text; to nurture a desire to read; and to develop lifelong learners who can use text information to satisfy personal needs and interests and fully and wisely participate in society—the value of literature becomes obvious. How are teachers to stimulate minds and hearts without good literature? How are students to explore ideas, come to understand the perspectives of others, grow in their thinking, and develop a love of reading without good literature? Literature nurtures the imagination, provides enjoyment, and supports the understanding of ourselves, others, and the world in which we live. Without authentic and compelling texts and meaningful instructional contexts, quality literacy instruction cannot happen (Raphael, 2000) and we cannot achieve the goals that we hold dear.

Literature-based instruction is influenced by three theoretical perspectives: reader response, cognitive-constructivist, and sociocultural. Reader-response theories had their beginnings with I. A. Richards (1929) and Louise Rosenblatt (1938). Prior to the work of Richards and Rosenblatt, literary theory focused primarily on the author and then on the text and largely ignored the role of the reader. Reader-response theories emphasized that what the reader brings to the reading process matters just as what the author brings to the process matters and that, without a reader, texts are merely marks on a page. The reader's experiences, feelings, beliefs, attitudes, and knowledge all influence his or her reading of a text and are, in turn, influenced by the text.

Authorities identify several groups of reader-response theorists, but it is Rosenblatt who has had the greatest influence on teachers, although it was not until the 1970s and 1980s that her ideas gained a wide audience. In Rosenblatt's view, a transaction between the reader and the text occurs during the reading process. The transaction is influenced, in part, by the stance that a reader assumes during reading. The reader can take a predominantly aesthetic stance or a predominantly efferent stance. When taking an *aesthetic* stance, the reader focuses on feeling states during the reading, the lived-through experience of the reading. Emotions, associations, ideas, and attitudes are aroused in the reader during an aesthetic stance. You probably take a predominantly aesthetic stance when reading a mystery novel—you are curious about who committed the crime, you worry about the safety of the hero or heroine with whom you may be identifying, your heart beats a little faster at the climax, and you are relieved when the mystery is solved. In contrast, an *efferent* stance is one in which the reader attends to information that he or she wishes to acquire from the text for some reason, either self-imposed or imposed by others. You likely take a predominantly efferent stance when reading directions for setting up a new gadget in your home. Your purpose is to gather data so that you can make all the right connections and have a fully operational piece of equipment at your disposal.

It should not be assumed, however, that efferent reading happens only with informational text and that aesthetic reading occurs only with fictional text. Have you ever experienced confusion about a character in a book and flipped back through the pages to remind yourself just exactly what his relationship is with the protagonist? You were engaging in efferent reading. Your purpose was to gather information and to ensure you knew the character's identity. Conversely, have you responded to an informational text by recalling experiences and feelings related to the topic? Have you ever had a visceral reaction to the content of informational text? If so, you were reading aesthetically.

A reader's stance falls along a continuum from aesthetic to efferent and changes from text to text, situation to situation, and moment to moment. It is influenced by many factors, including the text, the reader, the context, and—in the case of students—the teacher. When teachers focus on the information in texts, they promote an efferent stance: Students read to gather and remember information. When teachers encourage enjoyment of the reading experience and invite and accept personal responses to the reading; when they ask students to recapture the lived-through experience of the reading through drawing, dancing, talking, writing, or role playing; when they allow students to build, express, and support their own interpretations of the text, they promote an aesthetic stance. Unfortunately, teachers often use activities with their students that evoke only efferent responses (Beach, 1993). Although gaining information from texts is important, reader-response theorists argue that students should also have many opportunities to respond aesthetically to literature.

Teachers who are influenced by reader-response theories understand that readers bring different backgrounds, experiences, understandings, and attitudes to their reading. These educators believe that reading is an experience accompanied by feelings and meanings and that responses resulting from a transaction between the reader and the text are dependent, in part, on the stance a reader takes and the opportunities for response that teachers provide. They foster students' aesthetic responses to literature. They respect different interpretations of text, rejecting the notion of one correct response, and they support students in reflecting on and revising their interpretations by prompting them to revisit the text and discuss their ideas with peers.

Like reader-response theories, cognitive-constructivist views of learning emphasize the importance of the reader in the reading process (Graves, Juel, & Graves, 2004). According to cognitive-constructive views, readers are not empty vessels or *tabula rasas* but, rather, bring complex networks of knowledge and experiences with them to a text. They use their knowledge and experiences as they construct understandings of a reading selection, and because different readers bring different backgrounds, experiences, and purposes to their reading, no two readers construct exactly the same understandings. Cognitive-constructive theorists emphasize the active nature of reading. Meaning making is the result of cognitive work, with more complex or unfamiliar texts requiring more work if understandings are to be constructed. Teachers who are influenced by cognitive-constructivist views of reading provide time and opportunities for students to think about what they already know and to extend their knowledge networks in a variety of ways, including learning from those around them. They appreciate the subjectivity of the reading experience. They engage their students in activities that require them to actively process the text, for example, by considering ideas, organizing information, and making links among ideas in books and with their own lives.

The third group of theories relevant to the rich use of literature in the classroom are sociocultural theories. Based on the work of Vygotsky (1978), who asserted that children learn through language-based social interactions, sociocultural theorists believe that learning is fundamentally a social process and that interactions among learners are crucial. These notions are clearly germane to students' interactions with text. In fact, many reading researchers maintain that deep-level understanding of text occurs only through interactions with others (Morrow & Gambrell, 2000). Teachers who understand that it is through language exchanges that students organize thought and construct meanings provide many opportunities for students to work together. They structure their classroom environments and learning experiences to promote student interactions. They ensure that students engage in discussions and negotiate their evolving understandings and interpretations of text with peers.

Discussion is a mainstay of learning in a sociocultural perspective. Traditionally, classroom discussions have been highly centralized—the teacher decides what the students will talk about and facilitates the discussion. A more decentralized view of discussion—one that deemphasizes the role of the teacher—has been advocated by many educators for some time (Almasi, 1995, 1996; Au, 2003; Beach, Appleman, Hynds, & Wilhelm, 2006; Langer, 1995; Wiencek & O'Flahavan, 1994). In this view, discussions are led by students and guided by their responses to a book. Small student-led group discussions provide students with opportunities to attain social and interpretive authority and may increase participation from students who are reluctant to speak in teacher-directed situations (Raphael, 2000). Unfortunately, although widely promoted in the professional literature, peer-led discussions are rare in classrooms (Almasi, O'Flahavan, & Ayra, 2001).

**Technology**

Computer-mediated discussions are a recent alternative to teacher-led and student-led discussions. In these online discussions, students build their understandings of and share their responses to books with students from other schools, states, and even countries. These discussions provide all students with the opportunity to respond to the comments of peers and may allow students who feel marginalized to more fully participate in a discussion (Gambrell, 2004). All three forms of discussion—teacher-led, student-led, and computer-mediated—have a place in the classroom, and the value of each depends on the particular and varying goals for discussion.

The purpose of this book is to assist teachers in providing their students with meaningful experiences with literature. We offer a variety of activities that are rooted in reader-response, cognitive-constructive, and sociocultural perspectives. The activities honor the readers by acknowledging that their backgrounds, knowledge, and experiences influence their transactions with literature and by inviting them to respond both efferently and aesthetically. Additionally, the activities honor the active engagement required for meaning making by prompting thoughtful interactions with text. Also, they honor the crucial role of social interaction in the construction of meaning as they stimulate discussion and collaboration.

In the next section, we describe key responsibilities of teachers as they share literature with their students. Then, we identify questions that guided our thinking as we selected activities to include in this book.

## Teacher Responsibilities

**Technology**

**1.** *Know children's literature.* Familiarize yourself with a wide variety of children's literature, and keep abreast of newly published works. Spend time in libraries and bookstores. Browse websites that provide lists of award-winning literature, reviews of children's literature, and ideas for using literature. Visit author websites. (Several interesting sites are listed in the Appendix.) Ask your students and their families to share their favorite titles and authors. Talk to colleagues about books and consider establishing book clubs at your school site. It is difficult to share great literature with students unless you are familiar with it yourself.

**2.** *Provide students with access to a wide variety of children's literature.* Develop a rich classroom library that includes selections reflecting a wide range of interests, topics, and difficulty levels. Make available a variety of genres, including informational books, which are a scarcity in many classrooms (Duke, 1999; Yopp & Yopp, 2006). Research has revealed that the availability of reading materials in extensive classroom libraries and opportunities to choose books are key factors in motivating students to read (Guthrie & Wigfield, 2000; Palmer, Codling, & Gambrell, 1994; Worthy, 2000, 2002).

**3.** *Provide time for reading and talking about books.* The best-stocked classroom and school libraries mean little if the books are never removed from the shelves. Students must be given time to read. And, as we noted earlier, they must be given opportunities to talk about books. Not only are understandings socially constructed, but talk about books motivates students to read (Guthrie & Wigfield, 2000). Be a reader yourself, and share what you are reading. Teachers who are highly engaged readers create students who are highly engaged readers as they model their enthusiasm and strategic thinking about texts (Dreher, 2003).

**4.** *Plan for whole-group, small-group, and individual experiences with literature.* Whole-class experiences with literature contribute to the building of a community and offer opportunities for scaffolded instruction and guidance. Small-group experiences provide students with greater opportunities for interaction and negotiation of meaning. Individual reading of self-selected books respects student interests and choice and helps students develop independent reading strategies that underlie lifelong reading.

**5.** *At those times when you choose to provide group experiences with a work of literature, be sure to read the book.* Simple as it may seem, it is very important that prior to engaging students in a literature experience, you read the entire book yourself. It is not possible to plan meaningful experiences or respond to students' explorations without being familiar with the book.

**6.** *Identify themes, topics, or compelling issues in the book.* The themes, topics, or issues you identify will guide the experiences you plan for your students. Be prepared for the possibility, however, that during the course of discussion other ideas may emerge from the students that will take precedence over the ones you selected.

**7.** *Plan activities for three stages of exploration: before, during, and after reading.* Prereading activities should set the stage for personal responses to literature, activate and build relevant background knowledge and language, help students set purposes for reading, and spark students' curiosity. During-reading activities should support students' active engagement with the text, fostering comprehension and prompting personal connections and responses to ideas in the text. Postreading activities should encourage students to respond to the literature in personally meaningful ways and to think deeply about and beyond the literature.

**8.** *Establish an atmosphere of trust.* Students will honestly communicate their feelings, experiences, and ideas only if there is an atmosphere of trust in the classroom. You can promote trust by listening actively to the contributions of your students, respecting all student attempts to share, and allowing for a variety of interpretations of the meaning of a selection as long as the readers can support their ideas on the basis of the language in the text or their own experiences. Disagreements among students should be used to lead them back to the book to conduct a closer analysis of the author's words or to prompt them to identify and elaborate on their experiences and knowledge that may differ from those of their peers.

## Rationale for Selection of Activities for This Book

The following questions guided our development of and search for activities to include in this book.

**1.** *Will the activity promote grand conversations about books?* "Grand conversations" can be best described by contrasting them to the "gentle inquisitions" that take place in many classrooms (Bird, 1988; Edelsky, 1988; Eeds & Wells, 1989). During grand conversations, students are encouraged to think, feel, and respond to ideas, issues, events, and characters in a book. They are invited to express their opinions, and their opinions are valued. Personal involvement with the ideas contained in the book is encouraged, and individual interpretations are permissible as long as they are supported with data from the text. Grand conversations are similar to the discussions that occur in adult book groups in that the focus is on topics that are meaningful to the participants, and everyone is encouraged to contribute.

During "gentle inquisitions," on the other hand, the tone of the classroom interaction is one of "checking up" on the students. The teacher asks questions, and the students answer them. Although it is appropriate to assess students' comprehension, studies have revealed that a great deal of reading instructional time is spent asking students questions for the purpose of assessing their comprehension (Durkin, 1979; Wendler, Samuels, & Moore, 1989), and that higher-level reasoning activities, such as discussing and analyzing what has been read, are not routinely emphasized for students (Langer, Applebee, Mullis, & Foertsch, 1990). Allington (1994, p. 23) agrees that children "need substantially less interrogation and substantially more opportunities to observe and engage in conversations about books, stories, and other texts they have read."

The activities provided in this book can be used to stimulate grand conversations. They provide teachers with structures for encouraging students to express their ideas honestly and share their thoughts and experiences with their peers. Thus, they provide an alternative to the traditional question-and-answer discussion format that usually focuses on correctness, can discourage meaningful conversations, and often limits participation to the most verbal children in the class.

**2.** *Will the activity activate and/or develop background knowledge?* According to reader-response and cognitive-constructivist theories, what the reader brings to a work of literature influences his or her interaction with the literature. In fact, research reveals that a reader's experiences and knowledge provide the basis for comprehension of ideas in a text (Willingham, 2006, 2006–07; Wolf, 2007). Comprehension is said to occur only when a reader can mentally activate a schema—that is, some relevant organized knowledge of the world—that offers an adequate account of the objects, events, and relationships described in the text (Anderson, 1984). The following sentences illustrate this phenomenon:

*Jones sacrificed and knocked in a run.* (Hirsch, 2006)

*The notes were sour because the seam split.* (Bransford & McCarrell, 1974)

If you are a baseball fan or player and bring rich knowledge of the sport to your reading, you will have no difficulty understanding the first sentence. However, note the wealth of familiarity with the sport that the sentence takes for granted. In order to make sense of the sentence, you must have sufficient world knowledge to infer that it is about baseball and that Jones is at bat. You must further understand that baseball consists of innings and outs, that players run around bases on a field, and that the sacrifice Jones makes is one of getting out so a teammate can run to home plate and score a point. If you do not have that knowledge about baseball—and some readers don't—you no doubt had difficulty understanding the sentence.

Now, reread the second sentence. Observe that the vocabulary is not difficult and the sentence is short, yet you may not understand it. You might possess the appropriate background knowledge, but the authors have not triggered that knowledge for you. If we provide the clue that the sentence is about a bagpipe, do you now understand it? You probably do. Your knowledge of bagpipes likely accounts for all the elements in the sentence: the split seam, the sour notes, and the cause-effect relationship between the two. Failure to activate, or call to mind, an appropriate schema results in poor comprehension. An effective teacher promotes comprehension in his or her students by providing experiences that encourage them to access relevant knowledge prior to reading a text. If students do not have the relevant background knowledge, the teacher helps the students acquire the appropriate knowledge through real-world experiences, other text or media experiences, or interactions with peers.

Many of the activities described in this book, especially those recommended for use before reading, are ideal for activating and building background knowledge. They prompt students to think and talk about experiences they have had or to articulate their opinions on topics about which they will subsequently read. Students with limited background knowledge on a topic will benefit from listening to the comments of peers.

**3.** *Will the activity prompt students to use comprehension strategies?* Good readers engage in numerous strategies as they read (Duke & Pearson, 2002; Pressley, 2002). They identify goals, preview texts, and construct hypotheses. They check—and often change—their hypotheses as they read, make inferences, monitor their reading, and evaluate the text. They integrate their prior knowledge with material from the text, selectively read and reread, reflect on and summarize text, and consider the usefulness of the text. Good readers are active.

A great deal of research has demonstrated that children can be taught to engage in the strategies that good readers use and that instruction in these strategies results in enhanced comprehension. Specifically, research supports teaching students to make predictions and activate prior knowledge (Duke & Pearson, 2002), monitor their comprehension, use text structure to organize understanding and recall of text information, construct visual representations, summarize text information, answer questions about text, and ask questions about text (National Reading Panel, 2000; RAND, 2002). Additionally, evidence suggests that teaching students to coordinate use of these strategies in a collaborative, engaging context is particularly effective (Brown, 2008; Reutzel, Smith, & Fawson, 2005).

To teach students strategies, literacy experts recommend a model of instruction that involves a gradual release of responsibility from the teacher to the student (Roehler & Duffy, 1984). The teacher begins by providing an explicit description of the strategies, including when and how to use them. Then, the teacher models the strategies, thinking aloud for the students as he or she reads. Next, the teacher and students engage in the strategies together, and the teacher provides feedback as the students make attempts to use the strategies. The teacher gradually releases responsibility to the students, providing less instruction and feedback as the students become more independent. Finally, students use the strategies independently, with cuing and prompting from the teacher until they autonomously apply the strategies they are learning.

The activities in this book prompt students to utilize comprehension strategies. As students participate in the activities, they actively engage with text. They make predictions and read to confirm or reject their predictions; they monitor their comprehension, noting whether they are understanding the text and identifying where clarification may be needed; they use text structures such as story elements to organize their understandings of a text; they construct visual representations to depict relationships among ideas, events, and concepts; they summarize information in a variety of ways; and they answer self-posed questions and those asked by others. Further, the activities provide numerous opportunities for students to integrate the strategies as they work with their peers in building understandings of and responding to text.

**4.** *Does the activity promote higher-level thinking?* Many teachers are familiar with Bloom's (1956) taxonomy of educational objectives, a hierarchical classification system that identifies levels of cognitive processing or thinking. As originally conceived, the levels of the taxonomy from lowest to highest are knowledge, comprehension, application, analysis, synthesis, and evaluation. Recently, the taxonomy was revised in significant ways (Anderson et al., 2001; Forehand, 2005). First, the new taxonomy is two dimensional and includes knowledge categories as well as cognitive processes. The knowledge categories are factual, conceptual, procedural, and metacognitive knowledge. Second, the original cognitive processes were reconceptualized, reordered, and phrased as verbs rather than nouns. They are remember, understand, apply, analyze, evaluate, and create. The higher levels are considered the most important outcomes of education (Krathwohl, 2002), and attention to them is critical. Indeed, one of the characteristics of teachers whose students excel in reading is that they promote higher-level thinking (Graves, Juel, & Graves, 2004).

Analyses of educational practices, curricular objectives, and test items conducted in the decades following the development of the original taxonomy revealed a heavy emphasis in schools on the lowest level of thinking (Krathwohl, 2002). According to Bloom (1984), many students spend considerable time engaged in recognition or recall of information. Taylor and colleagues (1999) reported that a very small number of teachers in their national study asked higher-level questions about reading selections, and that when discussions occurred, which was rare, they primarily focused on facts. The most recent National Assessment of Educational Progress (Lee, Grigg, & Donahue, 2007) found that only 31 percent of fourth-graders and 29 percent of eighth-graders scored at the proficient level or above in reading. These levels require higher-level thinking such as extending ideas in text by making inferences, drawing conclusions, making connections, generalizing about topics in a reading selection, demonstrating an awareness of how authors compose, judging texts critically, and giving thorough answers that indicate careful thought.

The activities included in this book facilitate higher-level thinking. They provide opportunities for active interchange among students as they negotiate meaning. They encourage students to ponder, talk, and write about ideas that they have or will confront in the reading selection. They require students to compare and contrast characters and books, analyze relationships, support their opinions with examples from the text, and make connections with their lives or other texts. Many of the activities promote creative responses to literature.

**5.** *Will the activity provide opportunities for talking and writing?* Students' understandings and appreciation of a work of literature transform and expand when they listen to the perspectives, interpretations, and relevant experiences and knowledge of others. And, when students work to organize and articulate their own thoughts and reactions to a text, their understandings and appreciation change and deepen. Thus, providing students with plentiful opportunities to talk with one another as they engage with literature enriches the literary experience. Students learn as they talk.

Likewise, when students write—formally or informally—in response to literature, they reflect on impressions and ideas, reconsider initial reactions, discover faulty reasoning, gain perspective, and find language to give voice to their understandings. They formulate ideas and organize their thoughts. The very process of putting words on paper (or keying them into a computer) supports their thinking. They more closely examine and engage with the literature as they work to express themselves. Like talking, writing in response to literature enriches students' transactions with text.

The activities described in this book provide myriad opportunities for students to talk with one another before, during, and after engaging with literature. None is intended to be reproduced on paper, independently completed by silent students, and submitted to the teacher for a grade. Rather, the activities serve as springboards for discussion and are designed to inspire students to articulate their ideas and listen and respond to the ideas of others. Writing to explore and express ideas may precede, accompany, or be a natural outgrowth of literature experiences.

**6.** *Are the activities appropriate for a broad range of readers?* Few would argue with the notion that all students should have the opportunity to engage with good literature. Unfortunately, however, in their efforts to meet the needs of low-achieving readers, some teachers limit these students to short prose and to worksheets and activities addressing only low-level cognitive skills. These students often have neither the opportunity to share in rich literature experiences nor the opportunity to participate in the grand conversations about books that other students enjoy. Indeed, several decades of research reveals that students in low-ability groups typically receive less instruction and qualitatively different instruction than students in high-ability groups (Allington, 1980, 1984, 1994; Anderson et al., 1985; Au, 2002; Bracey, 1987; Walmsley & Walp, 1989; Wuthrick, 1990). Yet, research suggests that instruction involving the use of high-quality literature can make a significant difference in low-achieving students' literacy development and that these students need opportunities for higher-level thinking and discussions about books (Li, 2004).

Similarly, the most advanced readers are often not well served and are given tasks that leave them bored and unchallenged (Colangelo, Assouline, & Gross, 2004; Tomlinson et al., 2003). These students, too, need access to high-quality learning experiences that address their potential and maximize their opportunities for growth. Activities that emphasize thinking, exploration, problem solving, and decision making, and that allow for creativity are appropriate for these learners (Vaughn, Bos, & Schumm, 2007). Like all learners, advanced students need a curriculum that stimulates and inspires (National Association for Gifted Children, 2008). They need opportunities to engage with increasingly complex and abstract content that demands higher-level thinking.

One of the advantages of the activities presented in this book is that they can be easily and successfully implemented with a broad range of readers. Students with different levels of academic preparedness can participate in and be challenged by the activities.

**English learners**

**7**. *Will English learners benefit from the activities?* More than five million school-aged youth in the United States are not fluent speakers of English (NCELA, 2006). Unfortunately, like low-achieving readers, many English learners receive instruction that focuses predominantly on word identification and low-level skills. Some become adequate decoders but because opportunities to actively, thoughtfully engage with rich text have been limited, comprehension is a significant problem (Au, 2002).

Although the educational community still has much to learn about supporting the literacy development of English learners, there are several key understandings that can guide teachers as they support students' interactions with literature as well as their English language development. These include the importance of comprehensible input, the crucial role of social interactions in low-anxiety settings, the distinction between conversational and academic language, and the value of culturally familiar literature.

English learners will have the greatest opportunity to participate fully in classroom learning experiences, while simultaneously building proficiency in the new language, if teachers make the content and language of instruction more accessible—in other words, if they provide "comprehensible input" (Krashen, 1982). Comprehensible input can be provided through the use of realia (real, concrete objects), models, visuals such as photographs and drawings, hands-on activities, and graphic organizers. In addition, comprehensibility can be increased when content is familiar (August & Shanahan, 2006). You read previously about the role of background knowledge in reading. This notion is significant as you work with English learners (Droop & Verhoeven, 1998). Students are more likely to understand text if they already know something about the content or if it reflects their experiences and lives. The more familiar the content of a work of literature, the fewer are the demands on students' linguistic abilities. Thus, activities that draw on or build students' background knowledge prior to reading support the comprehensibility of the text.

In addition to providing English learners with comprehensible input, teachers should ensure that English learners have many opportunities to interact with others. Social interaction, fundamental for all learners, is crucial for English learners. Goldenberg (1996) noted that small-group settings stimulate active engagement from English learners, particularly when students are involved in what he calls "instructional conversations"—conversations that focus on joint meaning making, involve questions that have multiple responses, and encourage elaboration. Students have more frequent opportunities to talk, clarify language and ideas, and negotiate meaning in small groups. Language use is purposeful and authentic. Active interplay among participants who listen, respond verbally and nonverbally, and elaborate on one another's comments supports language and cognition. However, this active interplay will not happen unless teachers have created a nonthreatening, low-anxiety atmosphere, one in which students are willing to take risks as they experiment with language in order to communicate. Additionally, activities that spark students' interest and that value varied responses are more likely to invite participation.

Teachers who work with English learners need to be aware of the fundamental distinction between conversational and academic language (Cummins, 1994). Conversational language is used in informal social interactions. It is generally contextualized language, occurring in familiar face-to-face settings and supported by gestures, facial expressions, intonation, and the immediate communicative context itself. English learners typically develop conversational language, or basic interpersonal communicative skills, fairly quickly. On the other hand, cognitive academic language proficiency—communication that depends heavily on language, demands greater cognitive involvement, and is much less supported by interpersonal or contextual cues (i.e., it is decontextualized language)—takes much longer to acquire (Cummins, 1979; Goldenberg, 2008). Teachers who understand the distinction between conversational and academic language will appreciate students' conversational abilities while recognizing that they may not have the academic language that will allow them to engage in thoughtful interactions with content without support. Teachers who understand the difference between conversational and academic language scaffold instruction in such a way as to facilitate students' understanding and, at the same time, attend to the development of their academic language.

As important as comprehensible input, social interactions, and teachers' support of academic language are, many argue that unless students find "themselves" in books, they may experience "aesthetic shutdown" (Athanases, 1998, p. 275). Reading about people who share the same cultural and ethnic background facilitates personal connections with books and contributes to positive attitudes toward reading (Al-Hazza & Buchar, 2008; Hefflin & Barksdale-Ladd, 2001). Meier (2003, p. 247) noted that "not every book used in a multilingual, multicultural classroom needs to represent people of color or to incorporate linguistic diversity, but if bilingual children and children of color make up the majority of the class, then the majority of books used in the class should reflect that fact." Furthermore, teachers should use materials that present diverse cultural groups in an authentic manner.

The activities in this book support English learners' interactions with literature in that they contribute to comprehensible input by including nonlinguistic elements and drawing on and valuing students' background knowledge, provide opportunities for social interactions that motivate meaningful communication as students share their ideas and understandings, and acknowledge the difference between conversational and academic language by providing scaffolds for thinking and talking about books and extending academic language. Many of the examples throughout this book are drawn from multicultural literature, and the Appendix shares relevant websites.

English learners should not be excluded from opportunities to engage with literature. Literature provides exposure to rich language and powerful ideas that are worth thinking and talking about. And, shared literature experiences can contribute to building a classroom community where all members feel comfortable participating in the conversation.

**8.** *Are the activities appropriate for a differentiated classroom?* One of the joys of teaching is interacting with a wide range of students who have different backgrounds, strengths, needs, interests, and preferred ways of learning. Every class is a mix of learners, and each new academic year brings a new set of individuals. What an exciting profession teaching is!

As teachers embrace the diversity in their classrooms they recognize the need to differentiate instruction in order to best serve their students (Tomlinson et al., 2003). *Differentiation* refers to teachers' efforts to provide meaningful and appropriate instruction for the full range of learners in their classrooms. In differentiated classrooms, teachers consider who their students are—their readiness, interests, and approaches to learning—as they select and recommend literature, plan different ways for students to interact with and make meaning from text, and prepare experiences that help students demonstrate and extend their understandings. Teachers utilize flexible grouping strategies so students participate in a variety of group structures and with different classmates and for various purposes (Tomlinson, 2001).

What does differentiated literature instruction look like? If some students in a second-grade class are ready to read a chapter book independently, the teacher ensures that these students do so. If some fifth-grade students would benefit from more purpose setting and background-building activities, the teacher provides plentiful and appropriate prereading experiences for these students. If some eighth-grade students need more opportunities to think about character traits and others need more opportunities to explore themes, the teacher develops different prompts for their journal writing. Students read books that allow them to be successful but that challenge their thinking. They engage in activities that address their particular needs. They respond to books in ways that match or extend their interests and learning preferences.

The activities in *Literature-Based Reading Activities* are ideal for the differentiated classroom. They may be used with a range of literature. They represent a variety of ways to process literature before, during, and after reading, and they prompt the development of diverse products that expand and deepen students' thinking and that represent students' cognitive and affective responses to text.

## The Role of New Literacies

**Technology**

We live in a time of rapid change. In a very small number of years, we have transitioned from a world of paper, pencils, and books to one of a variety of information and communication technologies. Many students today are comfortable with e-mail, text messages, blogs, web browsers, presentation software, video editors, and much more. They use these tools to seek out information; to communicate with classmates, teachers, and others; and to share their learning with their immediate classroom community as well as larger—even worldwide—communities. We cannot imagine the technologies the next generations of students will experience and how these technologies will impact their literacy needs.

These new technologies are redefining literacy and literacy instruction (Leu, Kinzer et al., 2004). Students need new reading comprehension skills, for example, to effectively search for information on the Internet. They must be able to identify and utilize search terms appropriate to their goals, sort through large amounts of information to determine what is relevant and what is not, navigate from link to link, critically evaluate websites, and integrate information across sites (Henry, 2006). Teachers must broaden their conceptions of literacy to include the skills needed to locate, read, and analyze multilayered information on the Internet, and students must be supported in their efforts to communicate and gain information using new technologies. The term *new literacies* is used to describe the skills, strategies, and dispositions that are required for participation in a technological world.

New technologies and the new literacies that are required to fully exploit them have the potential to expand students' interactions with literature in powerful ways (Castek, Bevans-Mangelson, & Goldstone, 2006; Leu, Castek et al., 2004). One contribution made by the Internet is in the area of book selection. The Internet is a remarkable resource for locating books to read because students and teachers have nearly instantaneous access to lists of books. If students have enjoyed Newbery Medal and Honor Books, they may wish to check past and current winners by typing "Newbery Award" into a search engine and selecting one of several links that pop up. Students peruse the electronic list, and if a title looks interesting, they can search the title of the book and find a synopsis and, often, reviews of the book. Similarly, if students have a favorite author, they can search the author's name and find titles of other books he or she has written as well as information about the author. Some sites allow students to search databases of award-winning books by age of the reader, genre, and other categories. Access to information about books is literally at students' fingertips! Some websites share streaming videos of actors reading aloud favorite books and others provide free access to digital texts. Several of these sites are listed in the Appendix.

The instant access to information that the Internet provides can expand and enrich students' understanding of a book they are reading by allowing them to quickly learn more about the content, setting, or issues in the book. If students are reading a book about the building of the Great Wall of China, for example, they may wish to search for information about the wall. The increased knowledge they bring to the text will enhance their understanding of it and may deepen their appreciation of the hardships faced by the people who built the wall. Or, what they learn may answer or raise questions about the authenticity of the author's depiction of the times or region. A story set in a southwestern United States desert may prompt questions about the temperature, wildlife, and vegetation in the region. Students can turn to the Internet to seek answers to their questions and learn more about the harsh environment in which a character lives.

The Internet also gives students access to larger and more diverse audiences for their work and the capability to communicate and collaborate with students beyond their classroom. Students can publish projects related to literature on a classroom web page for family members to view. They can participate in virtual book clubs and share ideas with groups around the globe, becoming exposed to new perspectives that may result in new ways of thinking about a book. They can use blogs as interactive journals and engage in online literature discussions. They can utilize *wikis* to create, comment on, and revise collaborative projects. They can present reviews of or commentaries on literature by creating podcasts.

Additionally, new technologies provide students with ways to respond to literature. Students can download images and video into multimedia presentations. They can utilize interactive whiteboards or digital video technology to share understandings, dramatizations, interpretations, and extensions of literature.

The possibilities for the use of technology to enrich students' interactions with literature before, during, and after reading are nearly endless. We provide suggestions throughout this book for capitalizing on information and communication technologies. At the same time that these experiences enhance students' understandings of literature, they also support their development of new literacies.

## CONCLUSION

Literature should be at the heart of our literacy programs. Not only does it support many aspects of literacy development—language, comprehension, writing, attitudes, and perceptions—but it also provides an excellent context for deep thinking and personal response. Literature inspires us and informs us; it nurtures our imaginations; it moves us to laughter, to tears, and to action. In the remaining chapters of this book, we provide activities that support students' rich interactions with text.

# *Prereading Activities*

## *Prereading*

| Purposes | Activities |
|---|---|

**Purposes**

- To promote personal responses
- To activate and build background knowledge
- To develop language
- To set purposes for reading
- To arouse curiosity and motivate students to read

**Activities**

- Anticipation guides
- Opinionnaires/questionnaires
- Book boxes
- Book bits
- Character quotes
- Contrast charts
- K-W-L charts
- Semantic maps
- Preview-predict-confirm
- Concrete experiences
- Picture packets
- Picture carousels
- Quickwrites
- Quickdraws

**English learners**

The importance of engaging students in prereading activities cannot be overemphasized. Prereading activities can stimulate personal responses to text, activate or build relevant background knowledge and language, prompt students to set purposes for reading, and ignite an interest in the reading selection. In addition, they provide the teacher with helpful information about students' preparation to interact meaningfully with the reading selection. Although important for all children, prereading activities can be especially valuable for English learners and struggling or reluctant readers.

Prereading activities can promote personal responses to literature by signaling students that their knowledge, experiences, ideas, feelings, and beliefs matter and by prompting them to think about ideas in a book before reading about them. When students learn that what they bring to the text is valued, they are likely to continue to bring themselves to the text. When students think and talk about issues, events, or ideas in a reading selection before they read about them in the book, they may feel a greater sense of connection to the book and gain a deeper appreciation for the events, experiences, characters, and other book content.

In addition, activities conducted prior to reading a selection can serve to activate and build students' background knowledge on topics or concepts addressed in the book. As noted in Chapter One, activation of relevant knowledge is fundamental to comprehension. What readers already know about the topic of a text influences their understanding of the text. All students can benefit from activities that draw attention to and/or build relevant knowledge of a topic. As students engage in these activities with one another, knowledge is shared: Students draw on their own knowledge and learn from the knowledge of others. As readers, they will bring more to the text and, in turn, get more from it. Classrooms with children from diverse backgrounds are well positioned for rich interactions; multiple perspectives and different information and experiences related to a topic can be shared, enriching all students' knowledge.

Students who bring relevant language to the text, too, are more likely to interact meaningfully with the reading selection. Activities that highlight or build vocabulary and prompt rich discussions of text-related ideas can significantly impact comprehension and are highly appropriate for use prior to reading. As students articulate their own ideas, feelings, and understandings and listen to those of others, as they seek clarification while talking with one another, as they think about words in relation to a topic, as they collaborate to make word choices, and as they respond verbally to hands-on experiences, they are building their language in a setting that is purposeful and has communication as its focus.

Prereading activities are instrumental in helping students set purposes for reading. Students may read a selection to learn more about a subject they have been discussing, answer a personal question on a topic, discover how a character will handle a conflict, learn if their experiences and feelings about an issue align with those of a character, discover the relevance of a particular object in a selection, or determine if their predictions are correct. Having set purposes for reading, students more actively engage with the selection and comprehension will be enhanced.

Prereading activities also serve to spark students' interest in the reading selection. Discussions, sharing of experiences, and hands-on activities can arouse their curiosity about a selection. Students are eager to read the text to learn what happens, to see whether their hypotheses and predictions about the text are correct, or to discover what the author has to say about a topic and whether their personal questions are addressed. We see a heightened motivation to read a book when students have thought about issues in the selection. Motivation can be the difference between engagement and disengagement, between action and inaction. Reluctant readers, in particular, need teachers who know how to stimulate their interest in a reading selection.

In this chapter, we describe 14 activities that may be used prior to reading a book, a chapter, or a passage. The first activity, the *anticipation guide*, prompts students to think about and take a stand on issues or ideas that they will later encounter. *Opinionnaires/questionnaires* are useful for tapping students' knowledge and previous related experiences as well as their beliefs and opinions on a subject. *Book boxes, book bits,* and *character quotes* provide students with clues about a selection. They serve to arouse curiosity and invite speculation about the characters, events, themes, or content of the book. *Contrast charts* are useful for helping students generate ideas in contrasting categories. *K-W-L charts* provide a simple format for students to identify what they know about a topic and what questions they have about the topic before reading. *Semantic maps,* graphic depictions of categorical information, serve to build, activate, and organize background knowledge. The *preview-predict-confirm* activity gives students the opportunity to preview texts in order to make predictions about their language and content. *Concrete experiences, picture packets,* and *picture carousels* provide students with experiences or opportunities to explore objects or images related to content in a reading selection. *Quickwrites* and *quickdraws* prompt students to make connections between their knowledge or experiences and text ideas. Each of these activities can serve to pique students' curiosity about a selection, prompting them to approach it with questioning minds.

Prereading activities are a critical part of the instructional cycle and are used with the following purposes in mind:

- To invite students to respond personally to text
- To activate and build students' background knowledge on topics or concepts relevant to the selection
- To develop language
- To set purposes for reading
- To arouse students' curiosity and motivate them to read

Several of the activities in this chapter and throughout this book also support students' visual literacy, the ability to make meaning from images such as illustrations, photographs, maps, graphs, and diagrams (Yenawine, 1997). Visual literacy is increasingly important in our image-rich world, and it complements linguistic (or verbal) literacy, the making of meaning from written or oral language.

**English learners**

English learners can benefit greatly from the prereading activities shared in this chapter. The frontloading of language and knowledge that occurs through prereading activities is supportive of students' successful interactions with text. Each activity provides a means for all students to communicate their individual experiences or feelings. Students engage in purposeful use of language in a setting of acceptance. English learners listen to the language of peers, and their own language production is supported by group members as they all work to clarify ideas. Relevant vocabulary is developed in authentic circumstances. Further, background knowledge, important for all learners, is especially important for English learners because it may compensate for limited English language proficiency. Background knowledge contributes to the comprehensibility of the text input. In addition, prereading activities that ignite students' interest provide the motivation for students to be persistent in their efforts to read. Students may expend considerable energy on texts they have a desire to read, even when those texts are linguistically challenging.

Prereading activities are also particularly beneficial for struggling readers because they build pertinent language and background, promote authentic uses of comprehension strategies, and provide the motivation for students to engage with text. The motivational aspects of prereading activities also can be key in bringing reluctant readers to books.

Finally, it is important to point out that prereading activities offer the teacher an opportunity to assess students. What do the students know about the topic at hand? Have they had experiences that will support their understanding of the issues or topics in the text? Do they have relevant vocabulary? Do they demonstrate any interest or curiosity in the ideas they will encounter in the reading selection? By listening closely to students, teachers will learn how much support must be provided in order to ensure meaningful interactions with the reading selection.

## Anticipation Guides

An anticipation guide (based on Readance, Bean, & Baldwin, 1981) is a list of statements with which the students are asked to agree or disagree. The statements are related to themes, issues, or concepts in the reading selection, and an effort is made to develop statements that will result in differences of opinion and thus lead to discussion. This activity primes students for making personal connections with the text and sparks their interest as they consider their own opinions and those of their classmates.

**Technology**

Several statements are presented to the students by projecting them onto a screen, writing them on a whiteboard or chart paper, or distributing them as a handout. Students are provided time to consider and respond privately to each of the statements before making their opinions public. Then they share their agreement or disagreement with each statement by raising their hands, signaling with thumbs up or down, holding up an "Agree" or "Disagree" card, moving to a designated side of the room, or submitting electronic responses via individual transmitters to a classroom receiver. With an electronic response system, student responses are pooled and the group data are displayed. If desired, the teacher can access an individual student's responses and can save responses for later comparisons. A classroom projection system is necessary to display questions and results to the students. The students share reasons for their responses and are encouraged to comment on their peers' responses. If an atmosphere of trust has been established in the classroom, students with minority opinions will feel comfortable sharing their thoughts.

Another way to structure the activity is to provide each student with a set of statements written on individual small strips of paper. Each student sorts the statements into two groups: those with which he or she agrees and those with which he or she disagrees. Then the students meet in groups to share their sorted strips and discuss their reasons for sorting the statements as they did.

Asking students to consider statements such as *Very good people sometimes make bad decisions* can generate lively discussion and prompt students to explore and identify their own attitudes and beliefs as well as contemplate those of their classmates. Students gain an appreciation for a diversity of perspectives. When the students later encounter the issues they discussed in the reading selection, they are likely to respond at a deeper level than if they had not considered the issues before reading.

Anticipation guides for several books are presented on the next few pages. A brief summary of each book is provided for the teacher and is not intended to be shared with the students. Sample student responses are offered in Example 2.3

and in many of the examples throughout this book. We are not suggesting that these are "correct" responses. They are provided only so the teacher can more fully understand the activity. Student responses will, and should, vary. In addition to indicating their agreement or disagreement with statements in an anticipation guide, students may be asked to write a brief comment in response to each statement.

## EXAMPLE 2.1

- **Title:** *Teammates*
- **Author:** Peter Golenbock
- **Grade Level:** 1–4
- **Summary:** This book describes the prejudice experienced by Jackie Robinson, the first black player in Major League baseball. It highlights his courage and the support he received from Pee Wee Reese, a white teammate.

### Anticipation Guide

**Agree    Disagree**

_____  _____    1. Staying away from people who are cruel to you is a good idea.

_____  _____    2. When you are very good at something, people like you.

_____  _____    3. Sometimes one person can make a difference in the world.

_____  _____    4. If everybody is being cruel to someone, there's probably a good reason.

## EXAMPLE 2.2

- **Title:** *Tuck Everlasting*
- **Author:** Natalie Babbitt
- **Grade Level:** 4–8
- **Summary:** Ten-year-old Winnie Foster stumbles upon the Tuck family's secret: They will live forever. Those who drink from a spring in the woods near the Fosters' home—which the Tucks did inadvertently 87 years ago—cannot die. In this thought-provoking story, Winnie faces a number of moral dilemmas and ultimately accomplishes something important.

### Anticipation Guide

**Agree    Disagree**

_____  _____    1. It would be wonderful to live forever.

_____  _____    2. You should never do something that your parents have forbidden.

_____  _____    3. Some secrets are so important that it is acceptable to do anything in order to keep them.

_____  _____    4. People should have the right to sell products even if they are harmful.

_____  _____    5. It is OK to hurt one person to protect many.

EXAMPLE 2.3

- **Title:** *Dragonwings*
- **Author:** Laurence Yep
- **Grade Level:** 5–8
- **Summary:** An 8-year-old boy travels from China to the United States to be with his father whom he has never seen. There, he confronts prejudice and discrimination as well as his own misperceptions about Americans. He watches his father struggle toward achieving his dream to fly. The story takes place in the early 1900s and was inspired by the actual account of a Chinese immigrant who built a flying machine in 1909.

### Anticipation Guide

| Agree | Disagree | |
|-------|----------|--|
| X | | 1. It would be exciting to move to a new country. |

*I think you'd see a lot of interesting things in another country.*

| | X | 2. Discrimination and prejudice often work both ways between immigrants and native peoples. |

*Usually the people already living in a country don't like newcomers, but newcomers want to be friends.*

| | X | 3. A father has a duty to always protect his children from harm. |

*Parents should take care of their children, but eventually children must take care of themselves.*

| X | | 4. People should not spend energy working on unrealistic goals. |

*If it's unrealistic, it's stupid for someone to spend time on it. He should find another goal.*

Anticipation guides may be used again after a selection has been read. The format of the anticipation guide can be easily modified to include a single column for anticipation responses in which students put a plus or a minus symbol (or a smiling or frowning face) indicating agreement or disagreement, and a second column for reaction responses. Students complete the second column after reading the selection.

After completing the activity the second time, students may discover that their attitudes and understandings have changed as a result of their reading.

## Opinionnaires/Questionnaires

Opinionnaires/questionnaires (Reasoner, 1976) are useful tools for helping readers examine their own values, attitudes, opinions, or experiences before they read the book. Constructing an opinionnaire/questionnaire is very much like constructing an anticipation guide. The teacher first identifies themes, ideas, or major events around which to focus discussion. Then the teacher generates questions to tap students' opinions, attitudes, or past experiences related to those themes. Some items on the opinionnaires/questionnaires may be open-ended, whereas others may be more structured and offer students a checklist of possible responses.

The purpose of this activity is to facilitate students' thinking about their own attitudes and experiences related to selected issues, not to elicit "correct" responses. The teacher should be accepting of all responses and avoid valuing some opinions more than others.

We have seen teachers respond to students in a way that suggests there is a single correct response, and we have seen students become increasingly uncomfortable in these situations. It is apparent in these cases that the teacher is not truly interested in the students' opinions, and the teacher's behavior serves as a roadblock to the grand conversations the activity could have prompted.

The opinionnaire/questionnaire depicted in Example 2.4 provides a structure for students to talk about being different. When they subsequently hear or read the story *Stargirl*, they are more likely to appreciate the story events. Note that extra spaces are included so that students may insert their own ideas.

## EXAMPLE 2.4

- **Title:** *Stargirl*
- **Author:** Jerry Spinelli
- **Grade Level:** 4–6
- **Summary:** A new girl attracts much attention at Mica High School because she is so different—she wears unusual clothes, behaves in unusual ways, and has an unusual name. Leo Borlock falls in love with her the moment he sees her but soon tries to convince her to become "normal." *Stargirl* is a story of popularity and conformity.

### *Opinionnaire/Questionnaire*

1. People who are different from their peers
   - _____ should be avoided because they are strange.
   - _____ should be taught to be like everyone else.
   - _____ should be appreciated for being different.
   - _____ should be laughed at because they are different.
   - _____ are just trying to get attention.
   - _____ _____
   - _____ _____

2. To shun someone means to act like he or she does not exist. What would you do if people shunned you?
   - _____ Tell an adult.
   - _____ Try to convince them to talk to you.
   - _____ Ignore them.
   - _____ Change your behavior, clothes, or hairstyle to see if they like the new you.
   - _____ _____

3. In the first column, rate the behavior on a scale of 1 (least) to 5 (most) in terms of kindness. In the second column, indicate with a Y (yes) or N (no) whether the behavior is something you would consider doing.

_____  _____  Giving birthday gifts

_____  _____  Helping someone carry bags of groceries

_____  _____  Cheering for the opposing team in a sporting event

_____  _____  Teaching someone to dance

_____  _____  Spying on neighbors

_____  _____  _____

4. If you could choose a name for yourself, what name would you choose? Why?

_____

_____

**Technology**

Students may use the opinionnaire/questionnaire to poll others (such as students in other classrooms or parents) to discover what they believe. The data may then be compiled for class summary and analysis using paper and pencil or electronic spreadsheets. Summary numerical data and charts can be displayed with a classroom projection system or posted to a class web page.

EXAMPLE 2.5

- **Title:** *Roll of Thunder, Hear My Cry*
- **Author:** Mildred Taylor
- **Grade Level:** 6–8
- **Summary:** Set in the South during the Depression, this story relates the struggles of a black family and its encounters with hate and prejudice.

# *Opinionnaire/Questionnaire*

Listed below are a few incidents that make some people feel bad. Which of them would make you feel bad?

_____ When someone you love is ashamed of you

_____ When people call you names

_____ When people act as if they are better than you

_____ When you are punished for something you did that you should not have done

_____ When someone stares at you

_____ _____

_____ _____

What would you do if you were tricked out of a favorite possession by someone you knew?

_____ Cry.

_____ Tell your parents and ask for their help.

_____ Tell that person's parents and ask for their help.

_____ Tell all your friends so they won't be nice to that person.

_____ Get it back somehow.

_____ Pretend you didn't like the possession anyway.

_____ Decide you didn't deserve the possession.

_____ Trick that person out of something to show him or her how it feels.

_____ _____

_____ _____

If you were in a store and the clerk who was waiting on you stopped helping you and turned to assist two other people, what would you do?

_____ Wait patiently.

_____ Leave and go somewhere else.

_____ Leave and tell your parents.

_____ Complain to the manager.

_____ Demand that the clerk finish helping you.

_____ _____

_____ _____

A boy in your class is always bothering you, acting smarter than you, and getting into mischief. Which of the following describe what you would do?

_____ Feel sorry for him.

_____ Try to be his friend and help him change.

_____ Ignore him.

_____ Tell him you don't like his behavior.

_____ Hope someone catches him someday.

_____ Tell on him.

_____ _____

_____ _____

If he came to you for help, what would you do?

_____ Tell him "No way!"

_____ Help him.

_____ Laugh at him.

_____ Pretend you'd help him, then don't.

_____ _____

_____ _____

As with the anticipation guides, opinionnaires/questionnaires may be revisited after students have read the book. Students may examine whether their reponses have changed, and if so, why they have changed.

# Book Boxes

The book box activity stimulates thinking about a selection and builds anticipation as students are shown objects that serve as clues to a text's content. Students use these clues to make predictions about the reading selection.

The teacher begins by informing students that they soon will be reading a new book and that there are several objects in a box that are somehow related to the book. The teacher draws one object from the box at a time. Students identify the object—this is particularly important when it is unusual or unfamiliar—and in small groups talk about the object and begin to generate predictions about the content of the book. What does the object suggest about the book? After several predictions are shared with the entire group, a second object is drawn from the box. Students once again engage in discussion, first in small groups and then as they share their thinking with the entire group. As each new object is drawn from the box, students' predictions about the selection are extended or revised. After students have seen all the objects, they make final predictions that must account for each object. It is important that students are given ample time to talk with one another and to share their evolving visions of the selection. Listening to the experiences, knowledge, and thinking of peers supports all students as they consider the objects and possible relationships among them.

Examples 2.6 and 2.7 provide suggestions for objects to be included in book boxes for *The First Strawberries* by Joseph Bruchac and *The Invention of Hugo Cabret* by Brian Selznick. Objects may be drawn from the book box in any order.

Example 2.8 provides a format to record clues and predictions if the teacher would like students to record their thinking in writing. Students identify each object as it is revealed, engage in a small-group discussion, and record two predictions—individually or as a group—before their thinking is shared with classmates. Developing two predictions about the content of a text after each clue stretches students' thinking and encourages elaboration in their discussion as they consider alternatives that would account for each of the clues.

The book box activity is valuable for a number of reasons. Students bring their experiences and knowledge to discussions with peers, and students' mental activity becomes public as they generate and explain predictions and share their thinking with one another. The use of objects is motivating and provides nonverbal support for understanding. Also, higher-order thinking is demanded as students consider the relationships among a number of objects and evaluate the adequacy of their predictions as additional information is revealed.

EXAMPLE 2.6

- **Title:** *The First Strawberries*
- **Author:** Joseph Bruchac
- **Grade Level:** K–3
- **Summary:** This Cherokee legend tells the origin of strawberries. A woman, angry at her husband for his harsh words when she is picking flowers rather than cooking their meal, walks away from him. He follows her but cannot catch up to her. The sun helps the man by causing strawberries to grow along her path. She stops to eat them and their sweetness reminds her of the happiness she shared with her husband.

### Objects in the Book Box

Figurines of a husband and wife (wedding attire makes this relationship explicit)
A bunch of flowers
Some strawberries

EXAMPLE 2.7

- **Title:** *The Invention of Hugo Cabret*
- **Author:** Brian Selznick
- **Grade Level:** 4–6
- **Summary:** An orphan who hides behind the walls of the train station in early twentieth-century Paris and maintains the station's clocks, Hugo works to rebuild a mechanical man found by his father before his death. Hugo's efforts propel him into a world of thievery, friendship, magic, and early filmmaking. Part wordless picture book and part narrative, Selznick won a Caldecott Award for this unique, imaginative work.

### Objects in the Book Box

Mechanical toy
Black and white film
Clock
Gears
Screwdriver
Book about magic or a magic trick
Journal containing a few sketches of a mechanical man
Photograph of a train station

EXAMPLE 2.8

- **Title:** *Bananas!*
- **Author:** Jacqueline Farmer
- **Grade Level:** 2–5
- **Summary:** Readers learn in this informational and sometimes humorous text about the nutritional value of bananas, how and where they are grown and distributed, and their history.

## Objects in the Book Box

| | |
|---|---|
| Banana | Twine |
| Magnifying glass | Plastic bag |
| Fork | Apple |

**Clue #1:** *banana*

**Prediction #1:** *The book is about the importance of eating fruits and vegetables.*

**Prediction #2:** *This is a recipe book about different kinds of breads, including banana bread.*

**Clue #2:** *plastic bag*

**Prediction #1:** *People are shopping at a grocery store and are putting bananas in a plastic bag.*

**Prediction #2:** *Bananas are being placed in plastic bags to help them ripen faster.*

**Clue #3:** *fork*

**Prediction #1:** *Some people went shopping and brought home bananas in a plastic bag. They set the table with knives, spoons, and forks, and eat bananas as part of their meal.*

**Prediction #2:** *The book is about the different ways people eat bananas. After bringing home bananas in a plastic bag from the marketplace, people in some parts of the world cut them up and eat them with a fork.*

**Clue #4:** *twine*

**Prediction #1:** *Bananas have been rotting and have fallen to the ground. The farmers use special forks to pick up the rotting bananas and put them in plastic bags. They use twine to tie the bag.*

**Prediction #2:** *A worker has brought his sack lunch to a dusty location. He keeps his food and utensils in a plastic bag and ties twine around the bag to keep the contents clean.*

**Clue #5:** *magnifying glass*

**Prediction #1:** *Scientists are using magnifying glasses to inspect bananas for dangerous bacteria. They cannot handle the bananas so use forks to hold them. Any banana found to be carrying bacteria is put inside a plastic bag and the bag is tied closed with the twine.*

**Prediction #2:** *Some people fry bananas. The magnifying glass may be used to start a fire for cooking. The bag and twine were used to transport the bananas from a banana plantation to a marketplace. Someone has bought bananas and is cooking them. They will be eaten with a fork.*

**Clue #6:** *apple*

**Prediction #1:** *The book is about nutritious foods, including apples and bananas. Before going to a market, foods are inspected with a magnifying glass to see if they are carrying bacteria or poisons. The bag and twine are used to store bananas on the way to market. The book shares one way of eating apples and bananas—as part of a fruit salad. The fork is used to eat the cut-up pieces of fruit.*

**Prediction #2:** *This book is about conducting experiments with food. Apples and bananas are put in a plastic bag that is tied closed with a string and left to rot. The fork is used to mash the rotting food to get a better view of it. The magnifying glass is used to observe the decay and fruit flies.*

---

In a similar activity described by Wilhelm (2007), the teacher shares items that might be found in the pocket of a character. Students examine the items one at a time and work together to determine what they reveal about the character.

# Book Bits

Book bits are similar to book boxes in that bits of information from a reading selection are shared with students before they read. Instead of objects, however, sentences or phrases from the text are shared. This sharing of bits of text arouses curiosity and stimulates thinking about the text.

The teacher prepares for this activity by selecting sentences or phrases from the text and writing each on a separate small strip of paper. The teacher should select as many sentences or phrases as there are students so everyone can participate and make a unique contribution to a group sharing of information. The book bits should reveal enough about the text to support understanding, but not so much as to limit thinking and hypothesizing about the selection.

The students are given a book bit and told that the book bits are all from the same reading selection. Each student reads his or her book bit silently and reflects on it for a moment. The teacher should make certain that students are able to read their book bits and should assist struggling readers and English learners as needed to ensure their success with this activity. In some cases, teachers may wish to be selective about which strips are given to particular students. After reading their book bits to themselves, the students are asked to think about the impressions they are beginning to formulate about the reading selection and to write their initial thoughts. What might the selection be about? What do they think they know about any characters? What do they think is happening or will happen? Do they have any information about the setting?

At a signal, the students move around the room, find a partner, and read their book bits to their partners. No discussion occurs at this time. Students simply read aloud their book bits to one another. After reading, students move on to find new partners with whom to share their book bits. After students have had the opportunity to share with three or four partners (or fewer or more, depending on the size of the group), the teacher asks them to return to their seats and quickly write any new impressions of the text based on information they acquired by listening to their partners' book bits. At a signal, students again circulate around the room and share their book bits with new partners. The teacher should call time before students hear all of the book bits.

After a final opportunity to record ideas about the text, students meet in small groups or pairs to pool their information. Because each student will likely have acquired information that other group members did not, every student can participate in the conversation and make contributions to the discussion. The pooled information is recorded on a piece of paper. If the reading selection is narrative, the teacher may suggest that each group fold a piece of paper into thirds and record information and speculations in three categories: characters, setting, and plot. See Example 2.11.

After students have completed this phase of the activity, each small group shares its information with the entire class and the teacher records the information on a large chart, interactive whiteboard, or overhead transparency. Students may be surprised to learn of a character, setting, or plot element that their small group had not encountered in their sharing of book bits. Or, they may have information that supports the ideas generated by another group. Or, they may have put pieces of information together in different ways to reach different conclusions about the text. After the whole-group sharing, volunteers may read aloud or comment on their individual writing, which should reflect the evolution of their thinking and hypothesis generation about the reading selection.

If sentences are carefully selected, students will form a number of plausible impressions and hypotheses about the text. If the sentences have revealed too much, the students' responses will converge. Notice that in Example 2.9, the word *thunder* does not appear in any of the book bits. This was a deliberate decision on the part of the teacher. Had the word appeared in a book bit (or had the teacher shared the title of the book), the students' thinking would have narrowed very quickly and their opportunities to consider connections among the book bits and to build interpretations would have been limited. Instead, students formed a variety of hypotheses about the selection as they read their own strip and then gathered information from peers. Their initial impressions may have had to be abandoned in favor of new ones that better accounted for the information they were gathering, and their interpretations continued to be revised as they obtained more and more information from their peers.

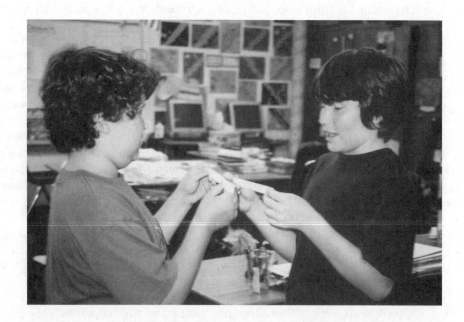

At the conclusion of the activity, students may be asked to compose a narrative (or expository work, if appropriate) that incorporates the information they gleaned from sharing their book bits and the follow-up discussions. Students should be challenged to include verbatim their own book bits in their writing.

## EXAMPLE 2.9

- **Title:** *Thunder Cake*
- **Author:** Patricia Polacco
- **Grade Level:** 1–3
- **Summary:** Drawing from her own experiences, Polacco shares the story of a young girl whose grandmother helps her overcome her fear of thunder. Babuska and her granddaughter locate the recipe and the ingredients to make Thunder Cake, which they complete just as the storm arrives.

### Book Bits

1-2-3-4-5-6-7-8-9-10

"I am here, child."

I was scared as we walked down the path.

"Eight miles, child," Grandma croaked.

"Now we have to get chocolate and sugar and flour from the dry shed."

We measured the ingredients.

This time it lit the whole sky.

"Only a very brave person could have done all them things."

## EXAMPLE 2.10

- **Title:** *Rules*
- **Author:** Cynthia Lord
- **Grade Level:** 4–8
- **Summary:** Twelve-year-old Catherine has a younger brother who is autistic. She loves him and creates rules for him to help him function in the world. She is also embarrassed by his behavior and resentful of the attention he receives from their parents. Accompanying her brother to a clinic, Catherine becomes acquainted with a paraplegic boy who uses word cards to communicate. Initially uncomfortable, Catherine hesitantly befriends the boy, adding words to his card collection and joining him at a dance. Topics of difference, disability, and acceptance are sensitively and realistically portrayed.

### Book Bits

Why can't the world be simpler, like it is for guinea pigs?

Don't run down the clinic hallway.

You can yell on a playground, but not during dinner.

It's fine to hug Mom, but not the clerk at the video store.

Don't stand in front of the TV when other people are watching it.

Mom says David'll never learn to talk right if we keep letting him borrow words.

I didn't know where to look, so I looked at his feet on his wheelchair footrests.

I rush outside to our porch swing, worried Mom's next words will be "Why don't you find Catherine and see what she's doing?"

You have to look underneath the words to figure out what he's trying to say.

On my way past Jason's wheelchair, I study a page of his communication book so my card'll match his others.

I turn the pages of Jason's communication book, reading through his cards so I don't repeat the words or phrases he already has.

I want to show Jason I'm sorry for not-looking at him the same embarrassed way I hate people not-looking at David.

"Remember the rule." I flip open the top of the aquarium. "No toys in the fish tank."

Everyone expects a tiny bit from him and a huge lot from me.

**Like. Guitar.**

**No. I mean. Catherine. My. Friend.**

I usually don't share my rule collection with anyone but David, but Jason's different.

"David doesn't learn from watching other people, so I have to teach him everything."

If someone is holding something you want, ask if you can have a turn.

I know she needs me to babysit sometimes, but I hate when she tells me he shouldn't be any trouble.

I tell myself it's a simple invitation to a birthday party, not a date.

## EXAMPLE 2.11

- **Title:** *Everything on a Waffle*
- **Author:** Paula Horvath
- **Grade Level:** 4–8
- **Summary:** When 11-year-old Primrose Squarp's father and mother are lost at sea, first Miss Perfidy (who charges by the hour), then Uncle Jack, and, for a short while, a foster family take responsibility for her. Primrose is certain that her parents are still living and trying to return home. She interacts with a variety of quirky characters and finds some comfort with Miss Bowzer, the cook and owner of a restaurant who serves everything on a waffle. Each chapter of this wonderful book of hope concludes with a recipe.

### Book Bits

I knew my parents were coming home someday but in the meantime I did miss my home.

"I'm not miserable all the time. Sometimes I get these bursts of joy."

I am eleven years old.

One June day a typhoon arose at sea that blew the rain practically perpendicular to our house.

The fishing boat never came back to shore.

Uncle Jack asked me if I minded moving but I could not shake the sense that none of it mattered very much.

When school started, my real troubles began.

A group of girls began to follow me and make jeering noises at me.

"Now that's true love and it's rare as rare can be."

At the end of September the rains began. There were fewer and fewer days when I could go to sit on a dock to wait for my parents without getting drenched.

The playground became less safe as my classmates lost patience with me completely.

We walked silently the rest of the way to the jail.

"I'm sorry, Primrose, but we've got a full restaurant tonight for some reason and it's a madhouse in here."

"And we're all so happy here in a small town."

"Everyone wants to sell," said Uncle Jack. "It's just a matter of price."

I heard the long blast of a truck horn and saw big wheels. Then nothing.

He was fighting those Child Protective Services folks tooth and claw for me, and calling constantly with progress reports.

The week before Christmas, Uncle Jack got out of the hospital and he and I took long therapeutic walks on the beach.

"Children who have had emotional upsets sometimes act out and need special care."

When Miss Perfidy answered the door, I noticed that she had her dress on backwards.

For the first time it occurred to me that Miss Perfidy, who must be in the neighborhood of 104 years old, might be failing.

"A fisherman on shore saw me and yelled and a bunch of men came running and untangled me and got me back onto the dock."

Then we formed the dough into rolls and Miss Bowzer lent me a pan to take them home in.

Then Miss Honeycutt started telling Uncle Jack that she never thought he should have been asked to take a child on.

"I don't know what you think the story of Jonah is about, Miss Perfidy," I said. "But to me it is about how hopeful the human heart is."

Miss Perfidy often stalked off when I was in the middle of a sentence.

In Coal Harbour there was whaling and fishing and the navy.

He pulled out a yellow macintosh and, with a face full of pity, handed it to me.

We entered the sheriff's office. Beyond his desk were two cells, clean but spare.

This is perhaps the easiest recipe of all.

| Characters | Setting | Plot |
|---|---|---|
| ■ *Miss Honeycutt*<br>■ *A teacher*<br>■ *A child of eleven*<br>■ *Uncle Jack*<br>■ *Miss Perfidy, an old woman*<br>■ *A sheriff* | ■ *Near the ocean*<br>■ *A small town*<br>■ *A fishing village*<br>■ *A restaurant*<br>■ *A jail*<br>■ *A school*<br>■ *The fall* | ■ *People are cooking.*<br>■ *Someone is a criminal.*<br>■ *There is a terrible storm.*<br>■ *A child is in danger.*<br>■ *A group of girls makes fun of someone.*<br>■ *Someone is having problems at school.*<br>■ *Someone's parents are gone.*<br>■ *An accident involving a truck happens.* |

# Character Quotes

Readers can learn much about the beliefs, feelings, and personalities of characters from the voices that authors give them. In this activity, small groups of students read a character quote and talk about what the quote reveals about the character before reading the text (Buehl, 2001). Many books have richly complex characters, and the teacher should select quotes that reflect the various facets of the character's personality. The teacher writes the quotes on separate pieces of paper or index cards and provides each group with one quote. In their small groups, the students read the quote and generate one or more words to describe the character. After each group records words based on its quote, the teacher asks students to share their quotes and words with the entire class. The teacher lists the words on a chart and informs the students that the words all describe the same character. Students discuss what they think they know about the character and often will share predictions about themes, issues, or events in the story as well. Students can return to the chart as they read the book and add or change words based on a growing understanding of the character.

An alternative to providing all groups with a quote from the same character is to give each group a small set of quotes from different characters. Each group discusses its character and shares impressions with the entire class. Another variation of this activity is to provide each group with two different colors of index cards—a yellow one with a quote from one character and a blue one with a quote from a different character. Students can think about the characters as well as their relationships to each other.

Students may be asked to write a paragraph that includes one of the quotes. Or, students may be challenged to write two paragraphs using the same quote in very different contexts.

EXAMPLE 2.12

- **Title:** *Joey Pigza Loses Control*
- **Author:** Jack Gantos
- **Grade Level:** 4–8
- **Summary:** Joey is excited to spend the summer with his father who has been absent from his life. Unfortunately, his well-intentioned father has serious problems and when he flushes Joey's ADHD medication down the toilet, things go awry and Joey must work hard to retain control of his life. This deeply moving and humorous book reminds the reader of human complexities and frailties.

### Sample Character Quotes
#### (Joey)

"I just want him to love me as much as I already love him."

"I want to listen to you, then I want you to listen to me, and go back and forth like people who want to know about each other."

"Dad is real nice. We had fun and he's putting me on his baseball team. He's buying me a glove and cleats."

"Are you okay? You're bleeding."

"I just don't play much with other kids. They tease me."

"Have you ever felt like two people at once?"

"I'm gonna need help. I really don't know what I'm doing."

"But I thought you told Mom you quit drinking, because she told me to call her if you drink and now it scares me not to call her."

"I'm taking a big chance on me and I need this to work."

"The only thing you have to worry about is that someone will yell at you. But if you are somebody like me, then having someone yell at you is no big deal."

"It was perfect! Awesome. The best day I ever had. I felt like the most normal kid in the world. Now I just want more and more of these days. A year of them. A lifetime of them."

"I want to have a conversation. It's been bothering me that I came all this way to see you but you never told me why you never came to see me."

## Contrast Charts

Contrast charts are used to facilitate students' thinking about ideas prior to encountering them in a text. Contrast charts are simple to develop, requiring only that the teacher identify theme-related contrasting categories under which students list ideas. For example, before reading about Karana, who lived alone on an island for years in *Island of the Blue Dolphins,* by Scott O'Dell, students list the advantages and disadvantages of living alone. As students consider two sides of an issue, they engage in higher-order thinking.

Contrast charts may be generated by the class as a whole, small groups of students, or individuals. We recommend that students be given a few minutes to individually consider the issues and record any thoughts that come to mind. Then, students may work in small groups to develop a group contrast chart by listing their ideas in two columns. Students benefit from interacting with one another as they listen to and explain ideas. Each group shares its chart with classmates. Contrast charts may be saved and revisited as students read the selection.

**Technology**

Students can develop contrast charts using markers and chart paper or a *wiki*, an electronic tool for collaborative authorship. After students or the teacher sets up a wiki web page for each group, students begin to construct their charts. One student might draw the two-column chart and list an idea or two. As other students in the group get on-line, they add to the chart or they modify or elaborate on ideas. Some students may wish to add clip art to their contrast charts to provide visual images of their ideas. Students construct their contrast charts prior to a whole-class discussion and then, if they choose, revise them after sharing their ideas and viewing contrast charts developed by other groups.

## EXAMPLE 2.13

- **Title:** *Alexander and the Terrible, Horrible, No Good, Very Bad Day*
- **Author:** Judith Viorst
- **Grade Level:** K–3
- **Summary:** Alexander has a horrible day when one thing after another goes wrong for him.

### Contrast Chart

Have you ever heard people say, "That made my day!" or "That ruined my day"? They are referring to events that happened that make them feel especially good or particularly miserable and cranky. List some things that could happen to you that could make your day either good or bad.

| Good Day | Bad Day |
|----------|---------|
| 1. | 1. |
| 2. | 2. |
| 3. | 3. |
| 4. | 4. |
| 5. | 5. |
| 6. | 6. |

EXAMPLE **2.14**

- **Title:** *Stuart Little*
- **Author:** E. B. White
- **Grade Level:** 4–6
- **Summary:** This story tells the humorous adventures of a two-inch mouse who is born into a human family.

## Contrast Chart

What would it be like if you were two inches tall? List some things that would be difficult to do. List some things that would be easy to do.

| **Difficult** | **Easy** |
|---|---|
| 1. | 1. |
| 2. | 2. |
| 3. | 3. |
| 4. | 4. |
| 5. | 5. |
| 6. | 6. |

EXAMPLE **2.15**

- **Title:** *Things Not Seen*
- **Author:** Andrew Clements
- **Grade Level:** 4–8
- **Summary:** Fifteen-year-old Bobby wakes up one morning to discover that he is invisible. His frantic parents—a physicist and a university professor—decide it is best not to tell anyone while they try to figure out what happened and how to reverse it. Officials become suspicious when Bobby stops attending school and his parents run out of excuses. Bobby tells a blind girl his problem and, with her help, the problem is solved.

## Contrast Chart

| **Advantages of Being Invisible** | **Disadvantages of Being Invisible** |
|---|---|
| *You can eavesdrop easily.* | *No one notices you.* |
| *You don't have to wash your hair, put on makeup, or wear nice clothes.* | *You can no longer participate in normal activities.* |
| *You can make faces at people and they won't know.* | *You don't matter to people.* |
| *You can go places you normally wouldn't be permitted to go.* | |

# K-W-L Charts

Another activity that helps students access their background knowledge on a topic is the K-W-L (know, want to know, learned) chart developed by Ogle (1986). The K-W-L chart is used before and after reading or listening to a selection that contains some factual content. Prior to the reading, students work in small groups or as a whole class to brainstorm and record in the first column of the chart what they know (or think they know) about the topic of the book. The pooling of information allows students to benefit from their collective background experiences and knowledge, sparks their memories of their own experiences and understandings, and prepares them for the literature. Sometimes student contributions to the *know* column will be challenged by classmates. In these cases, the teacher may want to allow students to reframe their statements as questions, or gently assist them in doing so, and write them in the middle (*want to know*) column of the chart. If misinformation is recorded in the first column, students will correct it after reading. Students next think about what they want to know about the topic and record their questions in the second column. When students generate questions, they set purposes for reading. Further, questioning will promote personal connections with text as students read or listen to find the answers to their own queries.

**Technology**

The discussions that occur as the first two columns of the chart are completed reveal to the teacher and students alike the extent of students' familiarity with the topic. If students' knowledge and relevant vocabulary are limited, the teacher may choose to develop their background before reading the text by reading aloud related—perhaps more foundational—texts, sharing video footage, or providing direct experiences with the content.

Example 2.16 shows the two columns students completed prior to their reading of the poem "Honeybees" in *Joyful Noise* by Paul Fleischman. Students recorded what they know about honeybees in the first column and what they want to know in the second column. After the selection is read, students record in a third column what they have learned about the topic and correct any inaccurate information listed in the first column.

## EXAMPLE 2.16

- **Title:** "Honeybees" from *Joyful Noise*
- **Author:** Paul Fleischman
- **Grade Level:** K–6
- **Summary:** This poem, one of a collection of poems about insects, describes the activities of the queen and worker honeybees.

### K-W-L Chart
*"Honeybees"*

| What We Know | What We Want to Know |
|---|---|
| *Make honey* | *How is the queen different?* |
| *Live in hives* | *Who lays the eggs?* |
| *Have a queen* | *How many are laid at a time?* |
| *Sting* | *How far away do bees fly from their hives?* |
| | *Why does the sting hurt so much?* |

**EXAMPLE 2.17**

- **Title:** *Marshes & Swamps*
- **Author:** Gail Gibbons
- **Grade Level:** 1–3
- **Summary:** After explaining the difference between marshes and swamps, the author describes various types of marshes and swamps, including how they are formed, where they are found in the United States, the life they support, and their importance.

### K-W-L Chart
*Marshes & Swamps*

| What We Know | What We Want to Know |
|---|---|
| Alligators and crocodiles live in swamps. | What is the difference between a marsh and a swamp? |
| Marshes and swamps are wet. | What lives in a swamp? |
| There are swamps in Florida. | What lives in a marsh? |
| Some people try to protect marshes and swamps. | Do alligators and crocodiles live in marshes? |
| Some birds need marshes and swamps to survive. | Are there snakes in marshes and swamps? |

It is important that the teacher restrict use of this activity to books that contain accurate information. Students should not be asked what they know and what they have learned about whales from a work of fiction that presents whales that chat with one another and have cute personalities. The wonderful story of *Gilberto and the Wind,* by Marie Hall Ets, anthropomorphizes the wind, using phrases such as *Wind likes my soap bubbles* and *Wind is all tired out* that clearly are inappropriate to include on a K-W-L chart. Therefore, the activity should not be used with this particular book.

By no means, however, should this activity be used exclusively with nonfiction. Many works of fiction have considerable factual content. In *Johnny Tremain,* by Esther Forbes, students learn a great deal about the Revolutionary War. In *Where the Red Fern Grows,* by Wilson Rawls, students learn about life in the Ozarks. In *Miracles on Maple Hill,* by Virginia Sorensen, students learn about the production of maple syrup. The teacher must be familiar with the reading selection and be confident that information presented about a topic under consideration is accurate before using it in a K-W-L chart.

It is likely that a number of questions generated by the students will not be addressed by the reading selection. Students should be encouraged to pursue answers to their questions by searching the Internet or exploring other sources. Ogle (1986, p. 567) said that this helps students recognize the "priority of their personal desire to learn over simply taking in what the author has chosen to include." A fourth column might be added to the chart (K-W-L-H) in which students record how they will obtain the information.

Technology

Another modification of this versatile chart, the KWLA, is the addition of a column on *affect* (Mandeville, 1994). This column can be completed before, during, or after reading. Before reading, students use the "A" column to share their feelings about the topic. During or after reading, students use this column to respond to the information they have learned—recording emotional reactions, indicating what they find most interesting in the selection, identifying parts in the reading they like the most or least, or noting why some information is especially important to them.

This linking of affective and cognitive domains has tremendous potential to spark students' interest in the factual information presented in many books, and Mandeville suggests that students who attach their own importance and personal relevance to information are likely to comprehend and remember the information better.

The discussions that are prompted by this activity can provide the teacher with information that may influence instructional decisions. For instance, if students have limited relevant background knowledge or vocabulary, the teacher may choose to provide instruction that builds understandings of concepts in the reading selection. If students demonstrate little enthusiasm for the topic, the teacher may plan activities to stimulate curiosity or help the students make connections between themselves and the topic that may motivate them to read. K-W-L charts provide teachers with information that can guide them as they provide differentiated instruction for their students.

# Semantic Maps

Semantic maps, sometimes referred to as *clusters* or *semantic webs*, are graphic displays of categorized information. They may be used to build key vocabulary and activate and organize students' background knowledge on a topic (Duke & Pearson, 2002). They give students anchor points to which new concepts they will encounter can be attached (McNeil, 1987). To make a semantic map, the teacher first writes and encircles a term that is central to the reading selection. In a selection about schools, for example, the teacher might write and encircle the word *school*. He or she next generates categories related to the central concept. For our school example, he or she might write *rooms, people,* and *studies.* Each is encircled and lines are drawn from the categories to the central concept of *school* to indicate a relationship. Then the teacher elicits from the students exemplars, details, or subordinate ideas for each of the categories. Within the category of *people*, for example, the students may list *children, teachers, principal,* and so on. These terms are written in the category circles. The teacher leads the students in a discussion about the terms and their relationships. Research suggests that this discussion is key to the effectiveness of the technique (Stahl & Vancil, 1986). After a map is generated, the class may want to save it to refer to during or after reading. At any point the map may be modified to reflect new information or ideas.

Another way to develop a semantic map is to have the students brainstorm and record the subordinate ideas after being told the central concept and then to group them into categories and label the categories. This approach is similar to Taba's (1967) list-group-label technique for concept development.

The use of semantic maps prior to reading has been found to result in better story recall in low-achieving readers than the use of the more traditional directed reading technique in which new content, new vocabulary, and the purpose for reading a selection are discussed prior to reading (Sinatra, Stahl-Gemake, & Berg, 1984). Their use is supported by schema theory described in Chapter One. Schemata (plural of schema) are networks of knowledge that readers store in their minds. Semantic maps help students tap those networks, integrate new information, and restructure existing networks. Because semantic

**English learners**

maps provide a visual display of concepts and the relationships among them and they tap, honor, and extend students' background knowledge and vocabulary, English learners are likely to benefit from their use.

Although semantic maps are used primarily to build vocabulary and activate and organize background knowledge, teachers may facilitate aesthetic responses to the text by including a category that taps students' emotional responses to the topic, as shown in Example 2.19.

**Technology**

Two software programs that many teachers and students find useful for creating maps are Kidspiration (for younger students) and Inspiration (for older students). These programs help users visually organize and communicate their ideas. The drawing tools on word-processing programs can also be useful for creating maps and other graphic organizers. Interactive whiteboards on which words and images can be dragged around make organizing and reorganizing information easy.

EXAMPLE **2.18**

- **Title:** *Charlotte's Web*
- **Author:** E. B. White
- **Grade Level:** 3–5
- **Summary:** Charlotte is a clever spider who befriends a pig named Wilbur. With the help of other animals, Charlotte saves Wilbur from a sure death.

**Semantic Map**

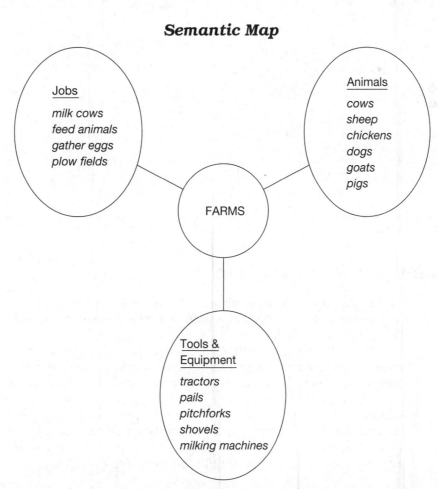

EXAMPLE **2.19**

- **Title:** *Surprising Sharks*
- **Author:** Nicola Davies
- **Grade Level:** K–3
- **Summary:** This picture book provides a wealth of information about sharks, including the numerous species of sharks, their anatomical features, and how they have more to fear from humans than humans do from them.

*Semantic Map*

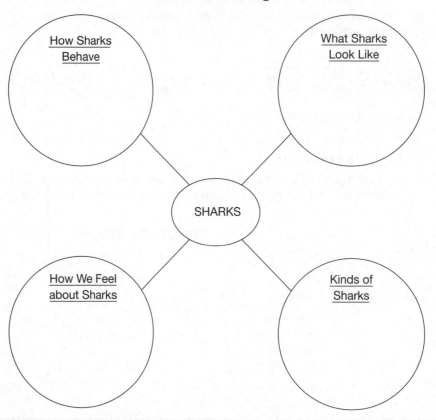

## *Preview-Predict-Confirm*

In this activity, students preview a book, make predictions about the language and content of the book, and confirm or reject their predictions after reading (Yopp & Yopp, 2004).

The activity begins with the students previewing a book by looking at each page as the teacher shares the book or by independently turning the pages of their own copies. After the students have briefly viewed each page, the teacher asks them to predict words they think the author may have used in the book without looking back at it. Three or four words are elicited, and the teacher asks for reasons the students think the words are in the book. For example, after looking at the pictures in Gail Gibbons's *Yippee-Yay!*, a book about cowboys, one student might say that he thinks the word *Texas* is in the book because cowboys live in Texas. Another student might predict the word *desert* is in the book and explain her contribution by stating that the pictures show the cowboys and cattle in the desert. A third student might explain predictions of *bandanna* and *boots* by stating that he saw a diagram in the book of cowboys' clothing that included these articles.

After several predictions are discussed, the teacher organizes the students into groups of three or four. Each group is provided with 30 to 40 (or fewer, depending on the ages of the students) small blank cards and the students are asked to predict as many words as they can and to record one word on each card. Students are told not to record words unrelated to the specific content of the book (such as *is, the, and*).

After the students have generated and recorded their words, they sort them into categories. Within their small groups, the students negotiate categories with one another, drawing on their observations and background knowledge to make decisions about which words fit together. Students often generate additional predictions during this opportunity to organize their words, and extra blank cards should be made available. Students label their categories and report their category labels during a quick share with the whole class.

The next step in this activity is to have each small group of students select three words from their cards: a word they think is common to all groups, a word they believe is unique to their group, and an interesting word. A representative from each group reveals his or her group's common word prediction, and the teacher notes overlap among the groups' predictions and asks why the words were chosen and what they reveal about the students' predictions about the book. What do they think the major ideas in the book will be? Next, each representative shares his or her group's unique word prediction, and, finally, each shares the group's interesting word. After each set of words is shared, the teacher asks questions about the word choices, such as, "What does the word have to do with the topic of the text?" and "In what context might the word appear?"

Finally, the students read the book or listen to it read aloud. As the book is read, students note whether their predicted words were used by the author. Whole-group or small-group discussion during or after the reading includes highlighting the author's use of predicted words, including how the words are used, as well as identifying words that might be added to categories in a group's collection. Example 2.21 shows words students thought were important to add after reading *The Moon* by Seymour Simon.

We note elsewhere that this activity supports students' comprehension in several ways (Yopp & Yopp, 2004). Foremost among them are that it contributes to vocabulary development and activates and builds relevant background knowledge as students think about words related to

a topic and then semantically organize them, as students discuss words and content with peers, and as they closely attend to the words and ideas of the author. It also promotes engagement in strategic reading as students generate questions about the book and establish purposes for reading.

**English learners**

Participation in preview-predict-confirm before reading benefits all students, and it is particularly useful for English learners. Having illustrations serve as the focus of a preview offers students a nonverbal source of information about a text. The small-group structure provides a relatively risk-free environment for students to share their vocabulary. Students' existing vocabulary is valued and all words are accepted and considered worthy contributions. For instance, after previewing the illustrations in *Sea Turtles,* by Gail Gibbons, students may offer words that range from simpler ones such as *water* and *fish* to more sophisticated ones such as *species, reproduction,* and *endangered.* Vocabulary is clarified and elaborated on as students spontaneously offer explanations for their word choices. In addition, students expand their understanding of words as they semantically sort them.

This activity provides an excellent opportunity for the teacher to assess students' readiness for a text. If students generate very few words related to the topic of the book after previewing pictures and discussing what they saw with peers, then the teacher will need to provide instruction and experiences related to the topic prior to asking the students to read the book in order to ensure meaningful interactions with the book.

## EXAMPLE 2.20

- **Title:** *Almost to Freedom*
- **Author:** Vaunda Micheaux Nelson
- **Grade Levels:** K–3
- **Summary:** A rag doll tells the story of her owner's escape from a Virginia plantation to freedom through the Underground Railroad. When accidentally left behind at one of the hiding places along the way, the doll is lonely until another runaway child finds it. The doll realizes it has an important job.

### Preview-Predict-Confirm

| Setting | People | Actions | Feelings |
|---------|--------|---------|----------|
| fire | men | work | scared |
| cotton | mother | pick | happy |
| stars | daughter | arrested | sad |
| night | father | watching | pain |
| boat | African | listening | |
| house | slaves | hide | **Doll** |
| basement | black | sleep | hold |
| fields | mouse | struggle | sew |
| dark | | cry | hug |
| ladder | | sneak | squeeze |
| | | row | |
| | | comfort | |
| | | climb | |

**Common word:** *doll*

**Unique word:** *sew*

**Interesting word:** *watching*

EXAMPLE **2.21**

- ■ **Title:** *The Moon*
- ■ **Author:** Seymour Simon
- ■ **Grade Level:** 3–6
- ■ **Summary:** Earth's only natural satellite, the moon is an object of great interest to scientists. The author shares information about the moon, its features and history, and the Apollo space program. Beautiful photographs accompany the informative text.

### *Preview-Predict-Confirm*

| The Moon | Studying the Moon | The Earth | Astronauts |
|---|---|---|---|
| moon | instruments | Earth | astronaut |
| craters | rover | big | Neil Armstrong |
| rock | radio | small | spacesuit |
| land | tool | light | first |
| round | camera | close | step |
| gravity | study | | space shuttle |
| dirt | look | **Survival** | footprint |
| | discover | oxygen | |
| | | air | |
| | | food | |
| | | water | |
| | | dead | |

**Common word:** *astronaut*

**Unique word:** *gravity*

**Interesting word:** *spacesuit*

**Words Added after Reading:**

| | | | |
|---|---|---|---|
| different | Apollo | flatlands | explosion |
| crescent | moonquakes | lava | feather |
| old | satellite | valleys | clover |
| phases | sun | mountains | |

# Concrete Experiences

Concrete experiences support students' understanding of a text by engaging them with the objects, concepts, or events discussed in the text prior to reading about them. Concrete experiences might include observations, investigations, or simulations. Before reading about light and shadows, for example, students might observe and record the movement of shadows on the playground. Before reading a book about simple machines, students might experiment with levers, pulleys, and inclined planes, talking about their explorations with peers in pairs or small groups. Before reading about mapmaking, students might draw their own maps of their classroom, school, or neighborhood, using the tools, skills, and language of a mapmaker.

According to Guthrie and Ozgungor (2002), concrete experiences—or real-world interactions—have both cognitive and motivational benefits. One cognitive benefit is that they cause students to activate background knowledge. As students observe, manipulate, and experience real objects and events, they often spontaneously describe prior experiences and knowledge related to the object or event and share their experiences and information with peers. When handling a collection of shells, for example, students might talk about collecting shells at the beach, share descriptions of shells they have seen, perhaps comparing them to the shells they are holding now, and discuss what they know about shells serving as homes for mollusks. This activation of background knowledge puts students in a state of readiness for new learning from text. Additional experiences with objects build background knowledge and develop vocabulary. A second cognitive benefit of concrete experiences is that they prompt students to ask questions, a strategy known to enhance comprehension (National Reading Panel, 2000; Nolte & Singer, 1985; Yopp, 1988). Questions serve as a beginning point for reading by creating a set of purposes for reading and cause students to be actively engaged with text as they read to find the answers to their questions.

Concrete experiences also have motivational benefits. Guthrie and Ozgungor (2002) argued that real-world interactions are intrinsically motivating and that the intrinsic motivation for these activities transfers to texts about the objects and experiences. Additionally, when students explore and experience real objects or events, they gain a sense of ownership over their new information. The results of students' observations and experiences become their personal knowledge, and a sense of control over one's knowledge and learning is integral to motivation (Skinner, Wellborn, & Connell, in Guthrie & Ozgungor, 2002). Any teacher who has witnessed children handling seeds, building bridges, or planning elections can appreciate the motivational aspects of these activities. This motivation carries over into reading about these experiences.

**English learners**

The use of concrete experiences is particularly supportive of English learners and is often recommended by authorities in second-language learning (Peregoy & Boyle, 2009). Use of realia supports students' efforts to learn new content because it provides something tangible to support their meaning making. Additionally, concrete experiences prompt purposeful and informal conversations in a low-anxiety setting, so English learners are more likely to engage in discussions. Indeed, all students make use of or begin developing relevant vocabulary as they talk with one another about what they are observing or experiencing.

Concrete experiences can be provided for many texts the students read and are especially appropriate for informational text. In the examples that follow, teachers provide students with opportunities to observe, touch, manipulate, and investigate real objects and discuss their experiences with peers prior to sharing related texts with them.

EXAMPLE **2.22**

- **Title:** *Pop! A Book about Bubbles*
- **Author:** Kimberly Brubaker Bradley
- **Grade Level:** K–3
- **Summary:** What are bubbles? Are they always round? How can you make bubbles? Why do they pop? These and many other questions are answered in this book about bubbles.

## Concrete Experiences

1. Have the students make a bubble solution. (A recipe is provided in the book.)
2. Provide bubble wands and allow the students to experiment freely with the solution.
3. After some free exploration, suggest that the students trying blowing slowly and quickly into their bubble wands and waving their wands in the air. Discuss what they observe.
4. Ask the students to describe bubbles. What is their shape? Can the students make other shapes? Do they see any bubbles that are attached to each other or other objects? What do they look like?
5. Ask the students what happens when they touch a bubble. What happens to a bubble if they do not touch it?
6. Ask the students where they have seen bubbles. Show them bubbles in a glass of soda, and ask them to describe what they see.
7. Ask volunteers to blow bubbles through a straw into various liquids, such as water, milk, and soda. What do they observe? Why do they think there might be differences?

EXAMPLE **2.23**

- **Title:** *A Drop of Water*
- **Author:** Walter Wick
- **Grade Level:** 3–6
- **Summary:** Beautiful photography supports the text in this informational book about water. Topics include surface tension, adhesion, capillary attraction, evaporation, condensation, and others.

## Concrete Experiences

The teacher can engage students in a variety of experiences that will support their understandings of the concepts in this book. We suggest one activity here, and others are provided by Wick at the end of his book. After participating in several experiences, the teacher may want to ask the students to think about observations of water they have made outside of the classroom, particularly as they illustrate the phenomena demonstrated in the activity below. Or, the teacher may write the word *water* in the middle of the board or chart paper and have the students create a cluster of what they know about water and questions they have about water.

*Water Drops on a Penny Activity:* Provide each pair of students with a penny, a cup of water, and an eye dropper. Ask the students to predict how many drops of water will fit on top of the penny, and then allow them to conduct tests and record their findings. They should see the water build up on top of the penny until the surface tension finally breaks, causing the water to spill over. When discussing the student's observations, use the terms *cohesion* and *surface tension* to describe these properties of water. (*Cohesion* is the attraction of water molecules to each other. *Surface tension* is the cohesion of water molecules at the surface of a body of water.) Encourage questions and explorations. How many drops might fit on a nickel or a quarter? Does it matter whether the students hold the eye dropper above the water collecting on top of the penny or touch the water with the tip of the eye dropper? Do other liquids have this same property?

## Picture Packets

Technology

Similar to concrete experiences are experiences with images (such as photographs, drawings, graphics, and maps) related to a reading selection. Before reading, packets containing images that have been downloaded from the Internet, cut from newspapers and magazines, or obtained from other sources are given to students to examine and discuss with peers. For example, before reading *Probing Volcanoes* by Laurie Lindop, small groups of students study photographs of dormant and active volcanoes, volcanic ash and rock, and volcanic craters. You can locate photographs by searching for "volcano images" on www.nationalgeographic.com. Students talk about what they know about volcanoes and what they see in the pictures, negotiating meaning and clarifying ideas. They generate questions about volcanoes, thus setting personal purposes for reading.

Before reading *Journey to Topaz* by Yoshiko Uchida, the story of one Japanese American family's relocation to an internment camp during World War II, students view photographs of the aftermath of the Pearl Harbor attack, Japanese American families leaving their homes under guard, an Exclusion Order announcing the relocation of all persons of Japanese descent, and barracks at internment camps. Students have both affective and cognitive reactions as they see children standing near barbed wire, watch towers, and armed guards. (The Online Archive of California has excellent photographs. Go to www.oac.cdlib.org, click on the images link, and type "Japanese internment" in the search box.)

*Dragon's Gate* by Lawrence Yep is a fictional account of Chinese immigrants' roles in building the transcontinental railroad. Before reading, students examine photographs of Chinese laborers and the conditions in which they lived, the ships on which the laborers traveled, the blasting of tunnels in mountainsides, and the driving of the Golden Spike; charts of the numbers of Chinese and other laborers; copies of newspaper articles; and maps detailing the route of the railroad. (One source of images is the Central Pacific Railroad Photographic History Museum at www.cprr.org.)

Multiple packets should be made so that every small group of students has access to the images and can view them closely. As students examine the packet contents, they think about what the images reveal about the book and what feelings they evoke. The teacher might ask the students to sort the images in some way that makes sense to them, or the teacher might lead the students in constructing a K-W-L chart or a semantic map about the topic of the book.

**Technology**

An alternative to preparing packets is to use presentation software such as PowerPoint or Keynote to share images with the entire class. Each image should be projected long enough that students can view it in detail. Students may discuss the images as they are viewed or after the entire presentation. Unless blocked by school or district firewalls, YouTube and TeacherTube are instant sources of videos that also can be shared. For example, a search of volcanoes on YouTube will yield dramatic footage of volcanoes around the world. A great source of maps and other images related to children's literature is www.googlelittrips.org/.

**English learners**

The use of images builds and activates students' background knowledge, arouses their curiosity, and stimulates personal reactions to the content. The images provide a nonverbal source of information, providing comprehensible input for English learners. At the same time, the peer group and teacher-facilitated discussions are instrumental in building learners' background knowledge and their academic language.

A writing extension of the picture packets activity is to distribute or project images and provide students with prompts that invite either efferent (What do you learn from this picture?) or aesthetic (How does this picture make you feel?) responses, or both. To allow for individual readiness, interest, and preference, the written response may take one of a number of forms, such as a list of words or phrases, a poem, or a narrative or expository passage. Students' informal drafts may be developed after sharing by providing students with the opportunity to revise, edit, and publish their writing.

## *Picture Carousels*

Picture carousels may be used to enrich students' background, spark their thinking and inference making, and elicit affective responses about a topic prior to reading. The teacher selects images that are related to the literature and posts them around the room. For example, photographs that capture the hardships of the Great Depression when people traveled the country in search of work are displayed before students read *The Train Jumper* (Brown, 2007), the story of a boy riding the rails during this period of American history. Images can be obtained from the Internet or other sources. Each displayed image is numbered, and students are given a guide that directs their attention to important aspects of the image or poses questions for students to consider as they examine the image. The guide is organized so that comments or questions correspond to each numbered photograph. Students individually or in pairs move around the room at their own pace, guides in hand, to explore each image and record notes. They are given ample time to view the images closely and thoughtfully. They then gather in small groups to discuss their responses to the questions and their reactions to the photographs.

**Technology**

An alternative to a guide with questions is an observation/inference (OI) chart, also designed to promote deep thinking and inference making about images or other nontraditional texts (Nokes, 2008). Each student carries a paper that has been folded in half to create two columns: one for observations the student makes as he or she examines the image and the other for inferences drawn. The student sketches arrows linking inferences with the observations that support them. Students will need many experiences making observations and differentiating them from inferences prior to using an OI chart. They will also need guidance developing inferences that are supportable from their observations.

Like many of the activities in this book, picture carousels are especially effective with differentiated instruction. All students participate in the picture carousel, but they read different books following their discussions. For instance, after students participate in the picture carousel for the orphan train (Example 2.24), some read Eve Bunting's *Train to Somewhere* and others read Joan Lowery Nixon's longer and more difficult *A Family Apart*. After books have been read, students share what they have learned and view the images again. Teachers can also differentiate by providing different response guides. Some students respond in writing to questions on a guide, as in Examples 2.24 and 2.25, and some may develop an OI chart. Others may create a sketch in response to each image. Still others may record a list of words that come to mind as they view an image.

## EXAMPLE 2.24

- **Title:** *Train to Somewhere*
- **Author:** Eve Bunting
- **Grade Level:** 2–4
- **Summary:** From the mid-1800s to the late 1920s, thousands of orphans in New York were taken by trains ("orphan trains") to the Midwest to be selected by families looking to adopt a child. This fictional account of one girl's experience is both tragic and hopeful.

Technology

- **Websites with Images:**

  http:/darkwing.uoregon.edu/~adoption/topics/orphan.html
  (The Adoption History Project at the University of Oregon)

  www.childrensaidsociety.org/about/history/orphantrain
  (Children's Aid Society)

  www.nebraskahistory.org/sites/mnh/orphans/ (Nebraska State Government)

  Or click on an images link on a search engine and type in "orphan train."

### *Picture Carousel*

**Image 1:** Photograph of a group of children standing in front of a train

Who do you think these children are and what are they doing?

Look at the children's clothing. Notice that the photograph is in black and white. When do you think the photograph was taken?

Look at the expressions on the children's faces. How do you think they feel? How do you feel as you view this photograph?

**Image 2:** Photograph of children looking out of train windows

Where do you think these children are going?

Do you think these children are with their families? Explain.

**Image 3:** Map showing the number of orphans taken to various states

What is the map showing us?

What do you think about this?

Which region of the country received the most children from the orphan trains?

**Image 4:** Poster soliciting homes for orphans

> What is the poster advertising?
>
> Why might children need homes?
>
> Who might choose to adopt one of these children?
>
> How does the poster make you feel?

**Image 5:** Close-up photograph of an older orphan seeking adoption

> How old do you think this girl is?
>
> Do you think she will be adopted? Explain.
>
> How do you think she is feeling?

EXAMPLE **2.25**

- **Title:** *Out of the Dust*
- **Author:** Karen Hesse
- **Grade Level:** 4–8
- **Summary:** Set in 1930s Oklahoma, this free-verse book reveals one family's ordeal with personal tragedy and the Dust Bowl catastrophe.

**Technology**

- **Useful Site for Images:** www.memory.loc.gov (the American Memory page of the Library of Congress website). Type "dust bowl" in the search box, or click on an images link on a search engine and type in "dust bowl."

### *Picture Carousel*

**Image 1:** Photograph of a blackened sky over a town

> What is your reaction to this photograph?
>
> Why do you think the sky in this photograph is dark?
>
> Where are the townspeople?
>
> How would you feel if you were in this town?
>
> What do you think will happen to the residents?
>
> Have you ever been involved in a natural disaster (such as an earthquake, tornado, flood)?
>
> What did you do? How did you feel?

**Image 2:** Photograph of a person covering his face from the dust

> Why is this person covering his face?
>
> What would happen if he didn't cover his face?
>
> What do you think he is thinking? What else?

**Image 3:** Photograph of a man and children running for shelter

> Why are these people running?
>
> How do you think the man feels?
>
> How do you think the children feel?
>
> What will they do when they get indoors?
>
> How does this photograph make you feel?

**Image 4:** Photograph of a car buried in dust

What are the first two words that come to your mind when you view this photograph?

How much of the car is buried in dust?

How long do you think it took for the dust to bury the car?

What will the owners of the car do?

Do you think the car will function?

**Image 5:** Photograph of crops destroyed by the dust

What happened to the crops in this photograph?

How long do you think it took to grow the crops? How long for them to be destroyed?

What are the implications of the destruction?

How do you think the farmers feel?

What do you think they will do?

**Image 6:** Map of the United States depicting the Dust Bowl region

In what part of the country did the Dust Bowl occur?

The Dust Bowl occurred in which states?

**Image 7:** Photograph of a car packed with furniture, luggage, and people

Where are these people going?

Why?

What will they do when they get to their destination?

What do you think they are hoping for?

How do you think they feel about leaving?

What have they left behind?

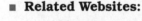

E X A M P L E  **2.26**

- **Title:** *By the Great Horn Spoon!*
- **Author:** Sid Fleischman
- **Grade Level:** 4–6
- **Summary:** Young Jack and his aunt's butler, Praiseworthy, stow away aboard a ship bound around Cape Horn to California in search of gold.

Technology

- **Related Websites:**

www.library.ca.gov/goldrush (the California State Library)

www.oac.cdlib.org (Online Archive of California, California Digital Library, University of California). Click on the images link and type "gold rush" and "gold rush sailing vessels" in the search box.

www.memory.loc.gov (the American Memory page of the Library of Congress website). Type "gold rush images" in the search box.

**Observation/Inference Chart**

| Observations | Inferences |
|---|---|
| Photograph 1: A group of men panning for gold<br>■ *The men are dirty.*<br>■ *The men are not smiling.*<br>■ *There are only men in the photograph.*<br>■ *They are using pans in running water.*<br>■ *There is no gold in the photograph.*<br>■ *The area is filthy.*<br>■ *The men are slumped over.* | ■ *They are working very hard and panning for gold is a difficult task.*<br>■ *Panning for gold is dirty, exhausting work.*<br>■ *The gold seekers did not have a lot of success.*<br>■ *Women did not participate in the panning for gold.*<br>■ *Conditions were not good.*<br>■ *They are tired and the work is exhausting.* |

# Quickwrites

Quickwrites serve to promote personal connections between the reader and the text, activate students' existing knowledge, and stimulate thinking on a topic prior to students' encounters with a reading selection.

Given a prompt from the teacher, students quickly write what they know about the topic or record their relevant personal experiences. For example, before reading *Throw Your Tooth on the Roof,* by Selby B. Beeler, students think about their own experiences in losing baby teeth. What became of the baby teeth? Many cultures have traditions surrounding the loss of a baby tooth: It is put under a pillow, buried in a garden, dropped down a mouse hole, or thrown on a roof. Beeler's book describes traditions from cultures around the world. Thinking and writing about their own experiences with lost teeth prior to reading stimulates students' personal connections with the topic.

Likewise, before reading about a Chinese American's wishes for his birthday in *Happy Birthday Mr. Kang,* by Susan L. Roth, students reflect on and write about wishes they have had for their own birthdays. Before reading about a young girl who has an unusual name in Kevin Henkes's *Chrysanthemum,* students briefly write something about their own name: its origin, their feelings about their name, or an incident involving their name.

After writing, students are provided an opportunity to share—in pairs, small groups, or as a class—their writing with peers. Conversations about the topic ensue and students may question one another for more detail, particularly as diverse responses are given. Example 2.27 provides sample quickwrites about waking up in the morning.

EXAMPLE **2.27**

- **Title:** *Mary Smith*
- **Author:** Andrea U'Ren
- **Grade Level:** 1–3
- **Summary:** Years ago, before the time when alarm clocks were common, people hired "knockers up" to awaken them in the morning. Most knockers up carried long poles and scratched on the windows of their clients' homes. Mary Smith used a peashooter to shoot dried peas at their windows.

## *Quickwrites*

*Prompt:* Take a few minutes to write about how you are awakened from sleep, especially on mornings when you need to rise early. What awakens you from your sleep?

**Student 1:**

*My mom has an alarm clock. Usually I hear it go off while I sleep, but I roll over and keep sleeping until my mother jiggles my arm and tells me it is time to get up. Sometimes she has to come back three or four times to get me out of bed. When that happens she grabs my feet and tosses them over the side of the bed and pulls me into a standing position. Sometimes when I'm anxious about something the night before, I automatically wake up early the next morning.*

**Student 2:**

*Usually my parents wake me up. Sometimes I hear my brothers talking in their room and that wakes me up. Some mornings when I want to be sure to get up early I leave the blinds on my windows open so that the sun shines through them in the morning. The way my room faces, the sun really makes my room light and that usually wakes me up.*

**Student 3:**

*My dog always sleeps with me. She usually wakes me up early in the morning because she wants to play and to be let outside. She whimpers and puts her nose right in my face. My dog is like my alarm clock.*

---

Quickwrites activate background knowledge and prompt personal connections as students reflect on their own knowledge and experiences and learn from the knowledge and experiences of one another. In this prereading activity, as in many, students discover that what they already know and what they have experienced matter in the reading act. Further, they appreciate that the contributions of all students are important and valuable. The more diverse the student population, the richer the pool of experiences and information that will be shared.

**English learners**

English learners may be encouraged to record their thoughts in the language that is most comfortable for them. If students are writing in a less familiar language, they should be given ample time to write. Further, teachers may want to provide all students with a moment of quiet reflection, or think time, prior to writing.

# Quickdraws

**English learners**

Quickdraws provide a different medium for students to reflect on and share their experiences or knowledge. Although appropriate for use with all students, quickdraws can be particularly effective with students who are new to the English language and students who are developing as users of written language.

Students are asked to quickly develop a sketch in response to a prompt. For instance, a teacher might provide students with a few minutes to quickly draw what they know about how electricity gets to their homes prior to sharing Barbara Seuling's *Flick a Switch: How Electricity Gets to Your Home.* Some children might draw electrical outlets, wires running through walls, and utility poles; others might draw transformers, electrical grids, wind turbines, dams, and nuclear power plants. After drawing, students are given the opportunity to talk about their drawings with one another. They are encouraged to revise or elaborate on their drawings based on their conversations with peers. Some drawings may be shared with the entire class by projecting them onto a screen or board using document projection technology. Students are encouraged to generate questions, which are recorded and displayed.

**Technology**

Example 2.28 shares one student's drawings of the front and back of a dollar bill before reading about the meaning of the symbols on U.S. currency. After the students drew from memory, they shared their drawings with peers and then refined their drawings. Then, the teacher shared several dollar bills for students to examine closely. Included in the example are some of the questions that students generated.

Quickdraws provide an opportunity for teachers to learn about students' experiences with a topic, their existing knowledge on that topic, and misconceptions they may have.

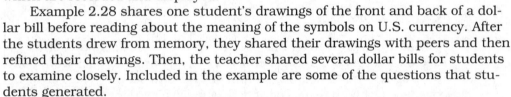

EXAMPLE **2.28**

- **Title:** *Money, Money, Money*
- **Author:** Nancy Winslow Parker
- **Grade Level:** 3–6
- **Summary:** The author provides interesting information about the meaning of the symbols and art on the paper currency of the United States. Readers also will learn about the individuals whose pictures are on the bills, the engraving and printing process, counterfeiting, and more.

## Quickdraw

*Prompt:* You probably handle or see money every day. In as much detail as possible, draw the front and back of a one-dollar bill without looking at one.

These questions were generated by the students after drawing, discussing, and viewing a dollar bill:

*Whose pictures are put on the paper money?*

*Why is there a pyramid?*

*What does the eye represent?*

*Why do some bills have an asterisk in the row of numbers?*

*Why is there more than one language on the bill?*

*What do those foreign words mean?*

*Why is there a city name on the bill?*

*What is the largest bill?*

*How is money made?*

*Why is the eagle holding arrows in its talons?*

---

## CONCLUSION

The fourteen prereading activities described in this chapter set the stage for personal responses to the literature, activate or build background knowledge, develop relevant language, prompt students to set purposes for reading, and motivate students to read. The activities involve students in thinking, discussing, responding, exploring, and shaping ideas. Students are likely to find the literature personally meaningful after engaging in these activities and to approach ideas contained in the books with greater interest, purpose, involvement, and appreciation.

Each of the activities also serves to prepare students for writing. When students consider issues, engage in discussions with one another, and reflect on and share their own relevant experiences, they find they have something to say. Writing is one means for them to continue the thinking that began with the activity. In addition, each activity may be flexibly employed to meet the needs of a range of learners.

### CHAPTER THREE

# During-Reading Activities

## During Reading

### Purposes

- To deepen comprehension
- To elicit personal responses
- To prompt students' use of comprehension strategies
- To enhance awareness and use of text structures
- To focus attention on language
- To facilitate thinking about characters, events, themes, and big ideas
- To promote collaborative building of interpretations

### Activities

- Literature circles
- Strategy cards
- Literature maps
- Character maps
- Character webs
- Character carousels
- Graphic organizers
- Character perspective charts
- Journals
- Character blogs
- Feelings charts
- Contrast charts
- Ten important words

There will be many occasions when teachers introduce a book and the students read it uninterrupted. During some literature experiences, however, teachers will choose to engage students in activities that facilitate and deepen comprehension of a selection and encourage personal responses to the literature.

Without comprehension, reading has not occurred and literature is of no value. Students' eyes may trail across lines of text, students may pronounce the words on the page, and they may even be able to tell us that Little Red Riding Hood's cape is red, but we cannot say they have *read* a selection unless they have constructed understandings of the selection. To read is to make meaning. Much of what students do before reading prepares them for meaningful interactions with the text. It is during reading, however, that students must actively engage with a text to build their understandings of it.

As we note in Chapter One, activities that prompt students' use of comprehension strategies—such as generating questions, creating visual images, summarizing, and making connections between their background knowledge and experiences and the text—enhance students' comprehension. Likewise, activities that guide students to notice and make use of text structures; focus their attention on the author's language; facilitate their thinking about characters, events, themes, and big ideas in the selection; and promote their collaborative building of interpretations of text with peers support comprehension. As students read and revisit sections of a selection and engage in during-reading activities, they actively process text.

During-reading activities also play a significant role in encouraging students' personal responses to literature. Although an efferent stance wherein students carry away information from a reading selection is important, literature is most powerful and most memorable when students approach it from an aesthetic stance. One way to promote an aesthetic stance is to provide an environment in which students are encouraged to respond personally to works of literature and to explore the responses of their classmates. During-reading activities that invite students to bring themselves to the literary experience, listen to the points of view of others, reflect on their own responses, and make connections between their lives and ideas in the text are critical to supporting aesthetic stances to reading.

This chapter describes 13 activities in which teachers may engage students during reading to deepen their understandings and responses to literature. *Literature circles* encourage students' strategic reading, negotiation of meaning with peers, and personal responses. *Strategy cards* also encourage strategic reading and promote a variety of responses to text. *Literature maps* enhance students' comprehension by assisting them in identifying and organizing information they find important or interesting. Literature maps can be used to focus students' attention on text elements, such as setting and characters; to call attention to language; and to allow for personal responses. *Character maps* are used for analyzing characters and their evolving relationships. *Character webs* and *character carousels* also enrich students' understanding of characters. *Graphic organizers* support students' understanding of text structures and content. *Character perspective charts* prompt students to think about story elements from more than one point of view. *Journals* and *character blogs* promote reactions and personal responses to reading selections. *Feelings charts* provide a format for identifying and describing different viewpoints. *Contrast charts*, described in Chapter Two as a prereading activity, are appropriate for all phases of the instructional cycle, and they are included here so the reader may see examples of their application

**Technology**

in another context and therefore gain a greater appreciation of their flexibility. The *ten important words* activity supports students' thoughtful interactions with text as they identify key words that capture the essence of a selection and build summaries of the content.

In summary, the during-reading activities in this chapter are offered with the following purposes in mind:

- To deepen comprehension
- To elicit personal responses
- To prompt students' use of comprehension strategies
- To enhance awareness and use of text structures
- To focus attention on language
- To facilitate thinking about characters, events, themes, and big ideas
- To promote collaborative building of interpretations

All students can benefit from participation in these activities. Advanced learners will appreciate opportunities for divergent thinking, critical examination of text, making connections to their own lives, identifying what they find most interesting in the text, and directing their own interactions with the text as they, for example, generate questions, lead discussions, or select important words and ideas. Lower-achieving readers, too, will find helpful the opportunities to negotiate meaning with peers, think about and make use of text structures to organize text content, examine text for evidence supporting their interpretations, use comprehension strategies for authentic reasons, and make connections between their lives and the text.

**English learners**

English learners will reap the benefits of participation in these activities for many of the same reasons. In addition, the use of graphics in some of these activities and the social interactions that are the heart of the activities when well used will support English learners' understandings. Because social interactions focus on communication, students' language is supported as they work to clarify ideas. At the same time, because some of these activities draw attention to the rich language that literature offers, English learners will have opportunities for building academic language proficiency.

## *Literature Circles*

Literature circles are temporary groupings of four or five students who meet regularly to discuss a work of literature that all members of the group have chosen to read. Each group decides when and how long to meet and how much of the selection to read between meetings. Group members assign themselves specific responsibilities for each upcoming discussion. These responsibilities are rotated. When a group has completed the book, it decides whether and how to share it with the entire class. Then the group is disbanded.

Daniels (1994) has provided several suggestions for group member responsibilities. Students may choose from among these, or the teacher may narrow the choices based on the text and students' needs. One responsibility is Discussion Director. This student develops discussion questions based on the reading and leads the discussion when the group meets. The Literary Luminary (for works of fiction) and Passage Master (for nonfiction) locate three or four brief passages to read aloud and respond to with the group. Choices may include interesting descriptions, humorous events, or important information; any reason for selecting a passage is acceptable. The Illustrator draws a picture or diagram that is related to the text. The Connector makes connections between the text and his or her own personal life, school life, events in the community, other writings, or anything else that the Connector feels is appropriate. The Vocabulary Enricher selects vocabulary from the text to share. Vocabulary choices may include unknown words, powerful words or phrases, or words that the author uses in an interesting way. The Travel Tracer's job is to record the movements of a character in the portion of text under discussion. This student writes a description or draws a map of a character's travels. The Investigator locates information that is relevant to the reading. This may be information, for instance, about the author, the setting, or the time period.

Each of the roles should be explained and demonstrated for students. Higher- and lower-quality responses, in terms of focus and thoughtfulness, should be modeled and discussed. Students should have opportunities to practice the roles and reflect on them over a period of time prior to being asked to perform them independently. Literature circles are not likely to be meaningful if the students have little preparation or experience with the roles.

Examples 3.1, 3.2, 3.3, and 3.4 show the notes of a Discussion Director, an Investigator, a Connector, and a Vocabulary Enricher for four different groups. These notes are not turned in to the group but, rather, are used to support the discussion.

Literature circles are useful for promoting students' responses to literature. By taking on a variety of roles in these groups, students develop appreciation for the multifaceted ways one might respond to a text. Students take ownership of their reading and the discussions and share what is meaningful to them. The literature circle experience allows students to make decisions about their reading, actively engage with the text and peers, explore ideas, and build and revise their understandings of the literature.

**English learners**

Further, the peer interaction that occurs in literature circles increases opportunities for meaningful communication using academic language, thus supporting English learners' language development. Additionally, literature circles provide a social learning context in which peers' scaffolding and modeling help students internalize and imitate literacy behaviors as they negotiate meaning and express their comprehension.

EXAMPLE **3.1**

- **Title:** *Mr. Popper's Penguins*
- **Author:** Richard and Florence Atwater
- **Grade Level:** 3–5
- **Summary:** Mr. Popper receives a penguin in the mail after sending a letter to an Arctic scientist. Mr. Popper and the penguin, named Captain Cook, have a number of hilarious adventures until the penguin's loneliness results in declining health. Soon Captain Cook is sent a mate, Greta, and nature takes its course, resulting in a house full of penguins. Mr. Popper takes the penguins on the road to perform their antics for audiences everywhere. Eventually, he makes the difficult decision to return the penguins to their natural habitat—and he accompanies them.

### Discussion Director
*(Chapters 8–9)*

*What were these chapters about?*

*What would you think if you were getting your hair cut and someone came in with a penguin?*

*What do you think will happen now that Greta is there?*

*What would you do if you had a pet that became mopey?*

*Do you think Mr. Popper and Captain Cook will get into more trouble?*

EXAMPLE $3.2$

- **Title:** *Olive's Ocean*
- **Author:** Kevin Henkes
- **Grade Level:** 5–8
- **Summary:** Martha did not know Olive well, so she was surprised when Olive's mother gave her a page from Olive's journal after the girl was killed in a bicycle accident. Martha learns from the journal entry that she and Olive had similar interests and that Olive had hoped they would become friends. Martha can't stop thinking about Olive while on a family visit to Cape Cod where she, on the brink of adolescence, learns much about herself and life.

### Investigator

**Technology**

*I was curious about the author because I know he's written a lot of books. I searched for him on the Internet and found out he has his own website. It's www.kevinhenkes.com. Some things I found out about him are that he loved drawing from the time he was really young and he also loved books. When he was in high school, he realized that he wanted to write and illustrate children's books for a career. He wrote his first book when he was 19. It's called All Alone. He says his books always begin with the characters and then grow from there.*

EXAMPLE $3.3$

- **Title:** *Painters of the Caves*
- **Author:** Patricia Lauber
- **Grade Level:** 4–8
- **Summary:** This text is rich with illustrations, photographs, and information about the ancient peoples who painted in Europe's caves.

### Connector

**Text:** *When the author discussed the dangers of cave exploration on the first page, I thought of the chapter in* The Adventures of Tom Sawyer *where Tom and Becky get lost in the long, dark passageways of the cave. Knowing what you are doing and having the right equipment is very important.*

**Self:** *I know firsthand how dark caves can be. I have been in caves, and last summer my family visited the Carlsbad Caverns in New Mexico. The caverns were HUGE. Human use of them dates back to prehistoric times.*

**World:** *We talk a lot about preserving natural environments. Caves and the ancient artifacts in them also need protection.*

EXAMPLE 3.4

- **Title:** *Bearstone*
- **Author:** Will Hobbs
- **Grade Level:** 5–8
- **Summary:** This Notable Children's Trade Book in the Field of Social Studies is another of Will Hobbs's coming-of-age stories of resilience and survival. Constantly in trouble, parentless 14-year-old Cloyd has been sent by his tribe to live with an old rancher in the Colorado mountains. There, he learns about life, love, and himself.

### *Vocabulary Enricher*
### (Chapter 4)

*I picked four words because I wasn't sure what they meant.*

**admonish**

*Pages 18–19:  "Old friends who dropped by would* admonish *him for not keeping up his strength, but as he told them, he was never hungry."*

*According to the dictionary,* admonish *means to caution, scold, or urge. I think here it means that his friends scolded him.*

**devoid**

*Page 19:  "Cloyd's large, round face was* devoid *of expression, unless it was the mouth turning dourly down at the corners."*

*The dictionary says that* devoid *means totally lacking. Cloyd had no expression on his face. His face was blank (except for his mouth).*

**dourly**

*Page 19:  "Cloyd's large, round face was* devoid *of expression, unless it was the mouth turning* dourly *down at the corners."*

*Dour means sullen (bad humor, resentment), gloomy, or stern. Cloyd's frown makes it look like he's in a bad mood.*

**potsherds**

*Page 21:  "Well, they say they lived all along the river—I've found a few grinding stones and whatnot, a few arrowheads and some* potsherds.*"*

*Potsherds are broken pottery fragments. The broken pottery and arrowheads are evidence that Indians did live along the river.*

---

## Strategy Cards

Strategy cards may be used to stimulate students' use of comprehension strategies as they listen to or read a text selection. The activity is similar to literature circles in that each student takes on a role such as Connector, Predictor, Summarizer, Questioner, Visual Image Creator, or Key Idea Identifier.

The roles are written on colored 3 × 5 cards, one per card, with all cards of the same color having the same role. Brief explanations or visual representations (such as a question mark and linked chains) of the roles may be written on the cards.

As with literature circles, teachers need to ensure that students understand the different roles. They should see good models, perhaps through a teacher think-aloud, and have ample practice before being expected to perform the roles independently.

The activity begins with the teacher randomly—or selectively, based on student needs—distributing the colored cards. In a single session, typically only three or four roles are used. Students think about their roles, then listen to or read a predetermined section of the literature. After the reading, students silently reflect on the literature and prepare to share their thoughts with peers. Students then meet with two or three classmates who have the same role; the color-coded cards make locating those peers a simple process. In their small role-alike groups, the students share their responses. After a few minutes, the teacher asks someone from a Summarizer group to share with the entire class. If other Summarizers wish to add to the first student's summary, they may. Next, the teacher asks students with a different role to share their thoughts. For instance, small groups of Visual Image Creators describe some of the images that came to mind as they heard or read the selection. After these have been shared and briefly discussed, a few of the Connectors offer connections they made to the selection. Students might be encouraged by the teacher or peers to briefly elaborate on their ideas. For example, if the students are listening to *Horses* (Simon, 2006), and one of the Connectors comments that every summer he visits his grandparents who care for horses at a ranch, the teacher and classmates might be interested to know more about his experience with and knowledge about horses. What they learn may enrich their understanding of or interest in the topic.

The students listen to or read more of the text until they reach the next predetermined stopping point. Again, they think quietly for a moment, formulating their responses, and then meet with others who have the same role. Students keep the same role for several rounds; their responses typically become richer as they move further into the text. Eventually, the teacher may ask students to trade their cards for one of a different color so they engage in a different strategy.

**Technology**

An alternative to distributing cards is to create a forum on a class website where students can post comments. This is most appropriate for longer books that are being read aloud over a period of time by the teacher or read silently by groups of students. Students locate on their class site the title of the book and click on it. There they find a list of the strategies. They post their responses to as many of the strategies as they wish and explore their classmates' postings. All students have the opportunity to contribute to the ongoing conversation.

**English learners**

Among the benefits of this activity is that comprehension strategies become transparent. Too often the processes that good readers engage in as they read are hidden. In the strategy cards activity, all students are prompted to engage with a text using a comprehension strategy and then they hear (or view) the thinking of others. This is powerful modeling for those students who may not be thoughtful, active readers and those for whom comprehension is difficult. Additionally, English learners or others with emerging language skills are supported as they first are given think time and then are provided the opportunity to work in a small group to discuss and contribute to the crafting of a response to share with the entire class.

EXAMPLE **3.5**

- **Title:** *Across the Alley*
- **Author:** Richard Michelson
- **Grade Level:** K–3
- **Summary:** Two young boys, one Jewish and one African American, live across a narrow alley from one another in Brooklyn. They are secret friends who hide their relationship because of prejudices in the community. At night, Abe loans his violin to Willie, who displays a talent for the instrument. Willie teaches Abe how to pitch a baseball.

(Responses after the first page)

**Response from a Summarizer Group:**

*A young boy lives across the alley from another boy. They don't play together during the day. At night they are best friends.*

**Responses from Questioner Groups:**

*Why don't they play together during the day?*

*Why do they only play together when nobody is watching?*

*How do you play together across an alley?*

*Where do they live?*

**Responses from Predictor Groups:**

*The boys will be caught and will get in trouble.*

*The boys' parents will be angry with them.*

*They eventually will get to play together during the day.*

**Responses from Connector Groups:**

*I live on an alley and there are a lot of kids. There is a lot of activity all the time. My alley doesn't look as narrow as the alley in this story.*

*In my small group, we talked about how when the one boy tiptoed out of bed after his Grandpa turned out the light that was like us. Sometimes we sneak out of bed when we are supposed to be going to sleep.*

## Literature Maps

Literature maps, described by Haskell (1987), provide a means for responding to literature while reading. Literature maps are constructed by folding a piece of paper (8½ × 11 or larger) into four or more sections and labeling each section with a category name. Categories may include "setting," "themes," "predictions," "vocabulary," "questions," "symbols," "imagery," "reactions," or the names of characters. Categories are generally identified by the teacher. However, some students may like to create their own categories as they are reading.

The reader's task is to write category-related information in each section as he or she reads a chapter or a book. For example, given a section labeled "setting," the reader jots down words, phrases, or sentences about the setting of the story. It is not necessary for the student to record all data relevant to a particular category. Rather, each student includes what he or she considers the most interesting or important information. A category such as "language" will yield diverse responses from students. Some students will write expressions they think are funny or unusual. Others may record words or phrases that confuse them. Still others may write descriptive phrases. As children bring their individuality to the literature, they will respond differently from one another.

**Technology**

After the maps have been completed by students, they are shared. The teacher or group recorder uses the tool bar on a word-processing program to insert a table with the appropriate number of cells into a blank document and projects the table onto a screen so everyone can see it. Or the teacher can draw a large map on a piece of butcher paper. The teacher asks group members to share responses from their personal maps and then she or he records them on the group map. Students may add to or modify their individual maps as they listen to the contributions of their classmates. If created electronically, the class literature map may be posted to a class web page so students can access it or to a wiki so they can add to it.

**Technology**

As Haskell (1987) pointed out, the benefits of this activity are many. First, students become more actively involved in their reading. They paraphrase ideas and identify important or interesting information while they are reading. Second, discussion is enhanced. Because children have taken notes while reading, they are better prepared to discuss the traits or behaviors of a particular character, for example. Third, the students have a record to which they may refer when writing about the reading selection. Fourth, students have the opportunity to hear what their peers think is important or interesting. Fifth, students begin to notice language that is appealing or effective. They begin to comment, "I like the way the author described that"—a first step toward internalizing and using effective language. Sixth, a map may be constructed at several points in a book, and students can trace the development of the plot or of characters.

An additional and very important benefit of this activity is that all students can contribute to a group map and feel success as their ideas are included. For example, given a particular character, some students may simply respond with physical characteristics such as "has red hair" or "is five years old," while other students may generate higher-level responses such as "is considerate of others," "is a listener," or "appears to have a good self-concept." All responses should be recorded. Thus, all students will feel comfortable responding and should have something to contribute to the group map and follow-up discussion. When higher-level responses are given, the teacher should ask, "What makes you think so?" The students then must draw on incidents from the reading selection that led to their conclusions. By verbalizing their reasons, the students are making their thinking overt.

It is important that the teacher avoid overwhelming the students with too many categories. Further, the teacher must recognize that some students may find this activity disruptive to their reading, particularly if they feel the need to stop quite frequently to record information. We recommend that students who find this activity disruptive be allowed to listen to or read a selection in its entirety first, then complete the literature map during a second reading. Or, students may mark pages containing information related to literature map topics with self-adhesive paper. They return to these pages later to complete their literature maps.

## EXAMPLE 3.6

- **Title:** *Ramona and Her Father*
- **Author:** Beverly Cleary
- **Grade Level:** 3–5
- **Summary:** Ramona's father loses his job, Ramona and Beezus go on a campaign to help him quit smoking, and Ramona practices acting so she can get a job on television commercials and earn enough money to help support her family.

### Literature Map

| *Ramona* | *Her Father* |
|---|---|
| *happy* | *lost his job* |
| *making Christmas list* | *worried* |
| *loves gummy bears* | *no fun anymore* |
| *wants to help family* | *patient* |
| *practices commercials* | *no money* |
| *gets burs in hair* | |
| **Beezus** | **Questions** |
| *grouchy* | *Will her father get another job?* |
| *loves gummy bears* | *Will her father be fun again?* |
| *going through a phase* | *Will Ramona be in commercials?* |

Literature maps are useful at any grade level. A kindergarten teacher may modify the activity by leading a discussion and serving as recorder on a group map. The teacher may wish to read the book aloud in its entirety first. Then, after rereading, the teacher may ask students to listen for particular information in order to construct a literature map. Students may be asked to pay attention to the traits and actions of certain characters or to the setting, for instance. The teacher records students' ideas in the appropriate sections on the map. The teacher may ask students to identify what they are thinking or feeling at particular points in the story. These comments are included in a "reactions" category.

## EXAMPLE 3.7

- **Title:** *Uncle Peter's Amazing Chinese Wedding*
- **Author:** Lenore Look
- **Grade Level:** K–2

■ **Summary:** Uncle Peter is getting married, much to young Jenny's dismay. The two have always had a very special relationship, and Jenny worries that her uncle will no longer have time for her. Many traditions of a Chinese wedding are described.

## Literature Map

| **Jenny** | **Uncle Peter** |
|---|---|
| *niece to Peter* | *"cool dude"* |
| *Chinese* | *getting married to Stella* |
| *Peter's "special girl"* | *fun* |
| *unhappy that Peter is getting married* | *happy* |
| *jealous of his bride* | *loves Stella and Jenny* |
| *wants Peter to play with her* | *kind* |
| *feels like "cosmic dust" next to Stella's "sun"* | *high school chess champion* |
| *tells her mother she will never leave her* | *track star* |
| | *mailman* |
| **Chinese Wedding Traditions** | **Questions** |
| *The bride's family gives the groom gifts.* | *Will Peter decide not to marry Stella?* |
| *Two hundred years ago the groom carried the bride on his back.* | *Will Stella be nice to Jenny?* |
| *For good luck, children go along to pick up the bride.* | *Will Jenny decide she likes Stella?* |
| *The groom bargains for the bride.* | *Will Peter continue to play with Jenny after he is married?* |
| *A tea ceremony welcomes the bride.* | *How much money is in the red envelopes?* |
| *Red paper packets are filled with lucky money and given to the bride and groom.* | *Are red envelopes given on other occasions?* |
| *The children jump on the bed, which is covered with candy. The number of children on the bed is the number of children the couple will have.* | |
| *They bow to show respect.* | |

EXAMPLE **3.8**

■ **Title:** *Hoot*
■ **Author:** Carl Hiaasen
■ **Grade Level:** 5–8

■ **Summary:** Roy Eberhardt's curiosity leads him to befriend a homeless boy and his sister and save some endangered owls from the proposed construction of a Mother Paula's All-American Pancake House. In the process, he learns to accept his new life in Florida.

## Literature Map
### (Chapters 1–2)

| **Roy Eberhardt** | **Curly** |
|---|---|
| *middle school student* | *bald* |
| *victim of bully on school bus* | *cranky and gruff* |
| *curious about running boy* | *upset about vandalism ruining construction schedule* |
| *new at school* | *supervising engineer at construction site* |
| *moves a lot because his dad works for the government* | *pretends he doesn't see owls* |
| *angry about moving* | |
| **Events** | **Questions and Predictions** |
| *Roy sees running boy from bus while Dana is squeezing his head.* | *Who is the running boy?* |
| *Curly reports vandalism on construction site to Officer Delinko.* | *Why is Roy so curious?* |
| *Roy sees the boy again, hits Dana, and jumps off the bus to chase the running boy.* | *Why isn't Roy more upset about how Dana treats him?* |
| *Roy gets injured by a golf ball.* | *I think that Roy will skip school to find the running boy.* |
| *He gets in trouble with the vice principal for hitting Dana.* | *Who is the girl and why does she tell Roy to mind his own business?* |
| **Setting** | **Interesting Language** |
| *school bus* | *A bald man is named Curly.* |
| *construction site* | *"cowgirl"* |
| *Trace Middle School* | *"whassamatter"* |
| *neighborhood* | |
| *golf course* | |

# Character Maps

Roser and Martinez (2005, pp. vi–vii) argued that it is "through characters that readers come to care about and connect with literature" and that understanding character "is so central to reading literature deeply and well, teachers need to ensure that students learn how to make sense of character," including traits, perspectives, motivation, feelings, and relationships. Character maps are used to help students understand characters as well as the relationships between characters.

**Technology**

After the students have read part of a book, the teacher or the students select at least two characters for analysis. Using software such as Kidspiration or simply sketching on a piece of paper, the teacher or students write each character's name at the top of a different circle or box and list information about each character in the appropriate space.

Next, the students draw an arrow from one character to another. Above and below the arrow, the students write words or phrases that tell how the first character feels about the second (e.g., "admires"), or what his or her relationship is to the second (e.g., "parent"). Several descriptors may be generated. A second arrow is drawn between these two characters, pointing in the opposite direction. Near this arrow the students write the second character's feelings about or relationship to the first.

**EXAMPLE 3.9**

- **Title:** *Charlotte's Web*
- **Author:** E. B. White
- **Grade Level:** 3–6
- **Summary:** Charlotte is a clever spider who befriends a pig named Wilbur and, with the help of other animals, saves him from a sure death.

### Character Map
(During Chapter 4)

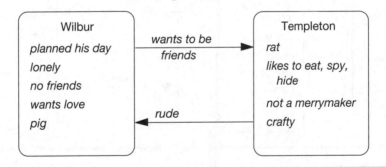

Character maps are useful in tracing the development of relationships. In the following example, two character maps are shown. The first was created by a class after reading the beginning of the story. The second was written as students finished reading the story. These maps allow students to analyze the changes in characters as well as the changing relationships between characters.

**EXAMPLE 3.10**

- **Title:** *Mike Mulligan and His Steam Shovel*
- **Author:** Virginia L. Burton
- **Grade Level:** K–2

- **Summary:** Mike Mulligan is sad because he and his steam shovel, Mary Anne, have been replaced by new, modern equipment. In order to find work, he goes to a neighboring town where he meets Henry B. Swap, who intends to trick him into doing work for no pay. The story ends happily when Henry B. Swap appreciates Mike Mulligan's skills and stories.

### Character Map
#### (Story Beginning)

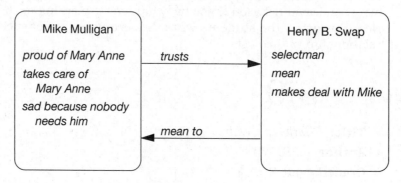

### Character Map
#### (Story Ending)

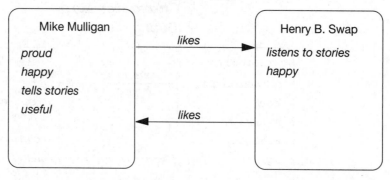

For more complex pieces of literature, several character maps might be developed. For example, in the book *Dragon's Gate,* by Laurence Yep, the young boy Otter greatly admires his Uncle Foxfire at the beginning of the book; is angry, bitter and disappointed with him later in the book; and then comes to understand and appreciate his uncle's courage and wisdom by the end of the book. The following three character maps illustrate changes that occur in the boy's perceptions of his uncle.

EXAMPLE 3.11

- **Title:** *Dragon's Gate*
- **Author:** Laurence Yep
- **Grade Level:** 5 and up

■ **Summary:** Otter, a young Chinese boy, flees his country to join his legendary Uncle Foxfire and his father in America as they acquire new skills and knowledge by working on the transcontinental railroad. They plan to use this knowledge when they return to China to conduct the "Great Work." Otter is surprised by the working conditions and prejudice he encounters.

## Character Map
### (Chapters 1–4)

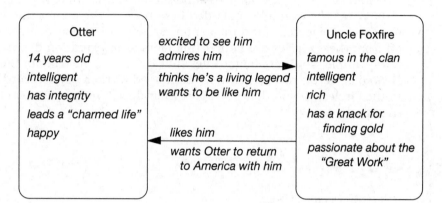

## Character Map
### (Chapter 10)

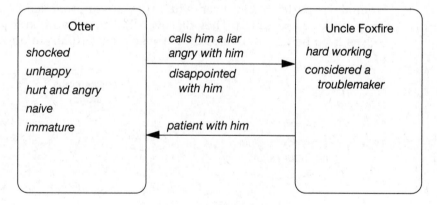

## Character Map
### (Chapters 24–25)

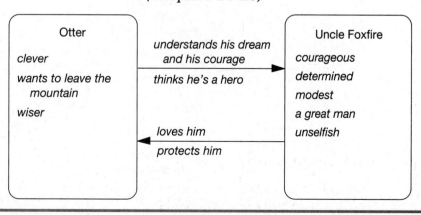

## cter Webs

Another activity for analyzing characters and facilitating discussions about them is character webbing. In this activity, students identify character traits and cite examples from the text as evidence. Bromley (1996) has noted that webbing enhances comprehension and learning, links reading and writing, and promotes enjoyment. Character webbing draws readers back to the text as they look for supporting examples, and so their interactions with the text are enriched.

Webs are very flexible instructional tools, and there are a great variety of web types. The examples included here have at the center the name of a character. Circles placed around the center circle contain character traits. Branching off from these circles are supporting facts or information drawn from the text. For example, students might infer that the doctor in William Steig's *Doctor DeSoto* is clever, nice, cautious, and a good worker. After recording these traits in the circles, the students support their decisions by citing incidents from the story.

## EXAMPLE 3.12

- **Title:** *Doctor DeSoto*
- **Author:** William Steig
- **Grade Level:** K–2
- **Summary:** A mouse dentist and his wife typically refuse to take dangerous animals as patients. However, when they are approached by a suffering fox, they make an exception. They discover that they had better protect themselves from being eaten, and they devise a clever plan to outsmart the fox.

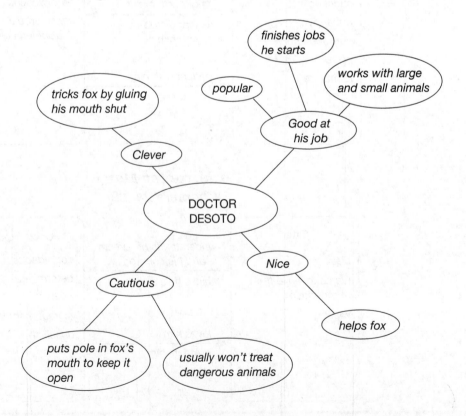

EXAMPLE **3.13**

- **Title:** *A Single Shard*
- **Author:** Linda Sue Park
- **Grade Level:** 4–8
- **Summary:** The young orphan Tree-ear lives under a bridge with Crane-man in twelfth-century Korea. Tree-ear longs to become a skilled potter. While admiring a piece made by the talented potter Min, Tree-ear accidentally breaks it. As payment, he works for the unfriendly Min. After proving himself worthy through hard work and loyalty, facing terrible danger on a journey to Songdo to show Min's pottery to the King's emissary, and losing his friend Crane-man, Tree-ear is finally welcomed by Min and granted the opportunity to learn to throw pots.

### Character Web

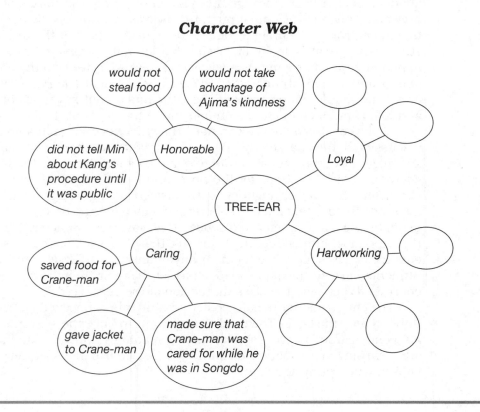

## Character Carousels

In Chapter Two, we described a prereading activity called picture carousels in which students circulate around the classroom viewing pictures and responding to prompts. In this similar during-reading activity, the teacher posts several charts in the room and writes at the top of each chart the name of a character from the book the students are reading. The students move from chart to chart and talk to peers about the character whose name appears on the chart. Unlike the picture carousel, students do not respond to specific prompts. Instead, they share whatever is important to them about the character. They may comment on the character's identity, appearance, or personality; discuss the character's role in the story; talk about how the character responded to different events; ask questions about the character's motives; or make predictions related to the character. Students record their thoughts on the chart and then move on to the next chart, where they read the responses of those who have visited the chart before them, and add new comments. Students are told that they may not repeat what has already been written. They rotate around the room until they have contributed to every chart. The teacher might allow students to freely move from chart to chart, or he or she may prefer to organize students into small groups that stay together and move to each chart at a signal.

Character carousels encourage students to reflect on the characters in a book they have read and to articulate, extend, and perhaps revise their ideas, understandings, and perspectives as they learn what their classmates think about each character. Because they cannot duplicate the comments recorded by previous students, they must push themselves to think deeply about the characters in order to make unique contributions to the chart. If the teacher has the students rotate at a signal, he or she should limit the time spent at each chart to no more than a few minutes so each group that rotates to the chart has the opportunity to contribute and so the activity moves at a fairly lively pace. However, time should not be so short that students do not have the chance to think and talk about a character before moving to the next chart.

At the conclusion of the carousel, the students engage in a whole-class discussion of the characters. The teacher might lead that discussion or he or she might ask groups of students to stand by a chart, review the recorded responses, summarize them for the class, and lead the conversation about that character. The teacher might choose to assign each group to a character by asking students to rotate back to their original chart, or he or she can invite students to select a character to discuss—their favorite character, the character they find most interesting, the character that they wonder the most about, the character that is most like them, or any other reason for selecting a character. Students move to the appropriate chart, share their thoughts with others at the chart, and then lead the class discussion of the character.

The charts should remain posted so students can view them as they continue to read the book. The teacher may want to have the students participate in a second character carousel after further reading so they can add to the charts after learning more about the characters. The charts may also serve as notes for subsequent writing activities.

## EXAMPLE 3.14

- **Title:** *Esperanza Rising*
- **Author:** Pamela Muñoz Ryan
- **Grade Level:** 5–8
- **Summary:** Esperanza lives on a large ranch in Mexico owned by her father. When tragedy strikes, she and her mother join servants as they cross the border into California and work on a farm in the central valley. Esperanza's mother becomes ill, the farm workers threaten to strike, and she survives the difficulties with help from friends and a willingness to start over.

## Character Carousel

| | |
|---|---|
| **Esperanza** | **Miguel** |
| 12 years old | son of servants of Esperanza's family |
| daughter of a wealthy landowner in Mexico | good friends with Esperanza |
| flees to California | likes trains |
| loved by her family | saved Esperanza's life |
| protagonist | kind |
| doesn't understand why her life has to change | hopeful |
| embarrassed by what she doesn't know | has a vision of how to get ahead in America |
| learns to work hard | determined |
| worried about her mother | angry with Esperanza for acting like a queen |
| stands up for herself and her family | |
| becomes sympathetic to Marta | |
| Will she strike? | |

| | |
|---|---|
| **Marta** | **Isabel** |
| makes fun of Esperanza | young girl |
| works on a neighboring farm | knows how to help the family and to do the work that needs to be done |
| tries to organize workers to strike | surprised at what Esperanza doesn't know |
| cares about people | teaches Esperanza |
| wants what she thinks is right and is willing to fight for it | wants to hear stories of Esperanza's former life |
| loves her mother | is hurt by unfairness at school |
| | simple things make her happy |

# Graphic Organizers

**English learners**

Graphic organizers are visual displays of relationships among ideas in a reading selection. They are used to help students organize information and to learn text structures. Graphic organizers support all students, and English learners in particular, by providing nonlinguistic representations of information in the text.

One type of graphic organizer is the story map. Most narrative text follows what is known as *story grammar,* or a set of rules by which a story is structured. Stories have characters and occur in settings. The main character has a goal or confronts a problem, engages in a number of activities to achieve the goal or overcome the problem, and, ultimately, attains a resolution. Strategies that make story grammar explicit, such as story mapping in which students identify and record elements of narrative text, help students create and remember stories and support comprehension development (Baumann & Bergeron, 1993; Dickson, Simmons, & Kame'enui, 1998; Dole, Brown, & Trathen, 1996; Leslie & Allen, 1999). Improved reading comprehension is more marked for less able readers (National Reading Panel, 2000).

Example 3.15 displays three maps for *Geraldine's Baby Brother,* by Holly Keller. First is a simple story map that helps students identify the beginning, middle, and end of stories. This is followed by more complex story maps that depict additional story elements.

E X A M P L E  $3.15$

- **Title:** *Geraldine's Baby Brother*
- **Author:** Holly Keller
- **Grade Level:** 1–3
- **Summary:** Geraldine is not happy that she has a new baby brother. She pouts and refuses to eat. The baby fusses and cries, and when Geraldine finds that she is the only one who can stop his crying, she decides he is not so bad after all.

### Story Map 1

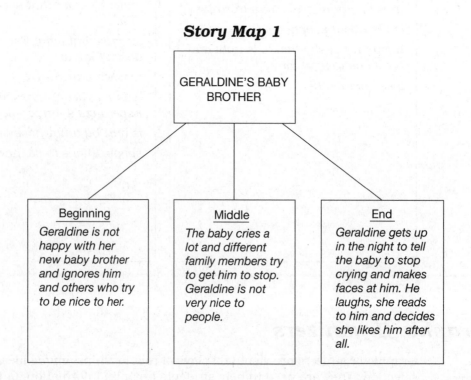

GERALDINE'S BABY BROTHER

**Beginning**
*Geraldine is not happy with her new baby brother and ignores him and others who try to be nice to her.*

**Middle**
*The baby cries a lot and different family members try to get him to stop. Geraldine is not very nice to people.*

**End**
*Geraldine gets up in the night to tell the baby to stop crying and makes faces at him. He laughs, she reads to him and decides she likes him after all.*

## Story Map 2

| Basic Situation | Complications or Events | Resolution |
|---|---|---|
| *Setting:*<br>*Geraldine's house*<br><br>*Characters:*<br>*Geraldine*<br>*baby brother*<br>*mother*<br>*father*<br>*aunt and uncle*<br>*Mrs. Wilson*<br><br>*Problem:*<br>*Geraldine doesn't like her brother.* | *Geraldine puts on earmuffs so she can't hear the baby.*<br><br>*Mrs. Wilson brings gifts for Geraldine and the baby. Geraldine doesn't open the gift.*<br><br>*The baby cries a lot.*<br><br>*No one can get the baby to stop crying.*<br><br>*Her parents forget to feed her lunch.*<br><br>*She goes to bed without dinner.* | *Geraldine gets up in the middle of the night to tell the baby to stop crying. She makes faces at him. He laughs and gurgles. She holds him and stays that way until morning.* |

## Story Map 3

**Setting:**

**Characters:**

**Problem:**

**Event 1:**

**Event 2:**

**Event 3:**

**Solution:**

---

Graphic organizers also support understanding of informational text. Informational texts often utilize one or more of the following organizational structures: description, sequence of events, cause-effect, problem-solution, and compare-contrast. Graphic organizers make these structures explicit to students, and students can use graphic organizers during reading to identify ideas in the texts as well as the relationships among them. Graphic organizers for the description text structure and sequence-of-events text structure are shared in Examples 3.16 and 3.17. Venn diagrams are useful for compare-contrast text structures and are shared in Chapter Four.

All of these graphic organizers are useful before, during, and after reading. We include them here because they provide a means for students to organize information as they read and reread a text. When they are used before reading, they provide a preview of text structure. When they are used after reading, they provide a scaffold for students' summaries of and reflections on text. Graphic organizers can be easily constructed with the drawing feature of a word-processing program or by using a specialized software program such as Kidspiration or Inspiration.

Technology

---

E X A M P L E   **3.16**

- **Title:** *Wonderful Worms*
- **Author:** Linda Glaser
- **Grade:** K–2
- **Summary:** The author shares interesting information about worms.

### *Graphic Organizer for Description Text Pattern*

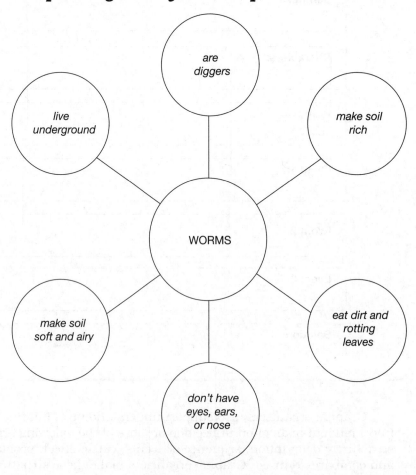

EXAMPLE **3.17**

- **Title:** *Waiting for Wings*
- **Author:** Lois Ehlert
- **Grade:** K–3
- **Summary:** This beautifully illustrated book shares the life cycle of butterflies.

### Graphic Organizer for Sequence of Events

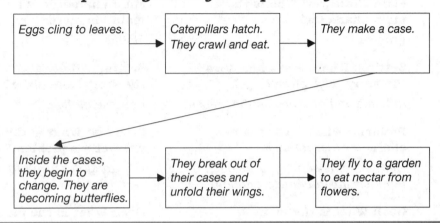

## Character Perspective Charts

Although story mapping has been demonstrated to enhance students' understanding of narrative text, Shanahan and Shanahan (1997) have noted that story mapping can foster a misconception that there is only one possible interpretation of a story. Character perspective charts maintain the benefits of story mapping while at the same time promoting multiple interpretations. Instead of focusing on a single character and his or her problems, in character perspective charting, the students are guided to consider the story from more than one viewpoint (Shanahan & Shanahan, 1997).

Two examples of character perspective charts are displayed in Examples 3.18 and 3.19. In these examples, the teacher prepared a two-column chart that outlines the elements of story grammar in each column. In one column, the students responded to the prompts from one character's perspective, and in the other column, they responded to the prompts from a second character's perspective. Small groups of children who read the same book engaged in conversation and completed the chart together.

EXAMPLE **3.18**

- **Title:** *Bread and Jam for Frances*
- **Author:** Russell Hoban
- **Grade Level:** 1–3

■ **Summary:** Little Frances is interested in eating only her favorite food—bread and jam. She refuses to eat other foods that Mother prepares. She even trades away the lunch Mother packs for bread and jam sandwiches that her classmates have. Mother decides to let Frances eat only bread and jam for a while, and Frances discovers that eating only one type of food, even if it is a favorite, is not as desirable as it seems.

## *Character Perspective Chart*

**Main character: Who is the main character?**

*Frances*

**Main character: Who is the main character?**

*Mother*

**Setting: Where and when does the story take place?**

*at home and at school in the present*

**Setting: Where and when does the story take place?**

*at home in the present*

**Problem: What is the main character's problem?**

*Her mother is serving foods other than her favorite bread and jam.*

**Problem: What is the main character's problem?**

*Her daughter won't try new foods.*

**Goal: What is the main character's goal? What does the character want?**

*She wants to eat only bread and jam.*

**Goal: What is the main character's goal? What does the character want?**

*She wants her daughter to try new foods and eat a variety of foods.*

**Attempt: What does the main character do to solve the problem or get the goal?**

*She trades her food for bread and jam.*

**Attempt: What does the main character do to solve the problem or get the goal?**

*She serves other foods at first, then she only serves bread and jam to Frances.*

**Outcome: What happens as a result of the attempt?**

*Frances becomes tired of eating only bread and jam and eagerly eats other foods.*

**Outcome: What happens as a result of the attempt?**

*Frances tries other foods.*

**Reaction: How does the main character feel about the outcome?**

*happy*

**Reaction: How does the main character feel about the outcome?**

*satisfied*

**Theme: What point did the author want to make?**

*Try new things.*

**Theme: What point did the author want to make?**

*The best strategy may be to let people discover some things for themselves.*

EXAMPLE **3.19**

- **Title:** *Walk Two Moons*
- **Author:** Sharon Creech
- **Grade Level:** 5–8
- **Summary:** In this award-winning novel, 13-year-old Salamanca travels across the country with her grandparents to the site where her mother, having left home to find herself, was killed in a bus accident. Salamanca struggles with the fact that her mother left and will never return. While on the road trip, she tells her grandparents the story of her neighbor, Phoebe, whose mother also disappeared.

### *Character Perspective Chart*

**Main character: Who is the main character?**

*Salamanca Hiddle*

**Main character: Who is the main character?**

*Phoebe Winterbottom*

**Setting: Where and when does the story take place?**

*on the road across the United States in the present*

**Setting: Where and when does the story take place?**

*in Euclid, Ohio, in the present*

**Problem: What is the main character's problem?**

*Her mother left the family and is not returning.*

**Problem: What is the main character's problem?**

*There has been a strange boy looking for Mrs. Winterbottom. Mrs. Winterbottom is behaving oddly. Mrs. Winterbottom leaves the family.*

**Goal: What is the main character's goal? What does the character want?**

*She wants to reach her mother by her mother's birthday.*

**Goal: What is the main character's goal? What does the character want?**

*She wants her mother to come home. She wants to find out who the boy is.*

**Attempt: What does the main character do to solve the problem or get the goal?**

*She goes on a car trip with her grandparents, following her mother's route.*

**Attempt: What does the main character do to solve the problem or get the goal?**

*She tries to convince others that the boy is a lunatic who has kidnapped her mother. She goes to the police. She tracks down the boy.*

**Outcome: What happens as a result of the attempt?**

*She gets to Lewiston, her mother's final destination, by her mother's birthday.*

**Outcome: What happens as a result of the attempt?**

*No one believes her. Her mother soon returns with the boy and everyone learns that the boy is her son.*

| **Reaction: How does the main character feel about the outcome?** | **Reaction: How does the main character feel about the outcome?** |
|---|---|
| *She accepts her mother's death and understands that her mother's decision to leave did not mean that her mother did not love her—the leaving was something separate from her love.* | *She is both happy and angry.* |
| **Theme: What point did the author want to make?** | **Theme: What point did the author want to make?** |
| *Don't judge a person until you've walked two moons in his or her moccasins.* | *Don't judge a person until you've walked two moons in his or her moccasins.* |

In a similar activity that combines story mapping with consideration of multiple perspectives, Emery (1996) has recommended a three-column chart. In the middle column, students record the story problem, a list of important events that occur in the story, and the resolution. A different character's name is put at the top of each of the two remaining columns. Students engage in a discussion about the characters' perspectives on each of the elements listed in the middle column. Their ideas are recorded in the appropriate column immediately across from each of the story elements.

# *Journals*

Journal writing in response to a reading selection helps to move both younger and older students beyond literal comprehension to a more complete understanding of the content of a book (Barone, 1989) and encourages personal, thoughtful engagement with books (Fuhler, 1994). There are many types of journals. Double-entry journals, reading logs, and partner journals are described here.

The purpose of a double-entry journal is to allow students to select passages they find meaningful in a reading selection and then to write about why those passages are meaningful. Students may use 8½ × 11 lined paper that has been folded in half lengthwise or create a two-column table with a word-processing program. In the left column, the student summarizes interesting information or copies verbatim a sentence or paragraph of his of her own choosing from the reading selection and records the page number. Directly across from the text information or quote, in the right column, the student reacts to the passage. Selections and responses will vary widely. Some passages may be selected because they are funny or use interesting language. Others may be selected because they touch the student's heart or remind the student of experiences in his or her own life.

This activity encourages interaction between the selection and the students and gives each student a chance to identify what is meaningful to him or her. Students may choose to share their responses with one another or to keep them private. The double-entry journal may be used effectively with children as young as first-graders (Barone, 1990).

EXAMPLE 3.20

- **Title:** *Zzz . . . The Most Interesting Book You'll Ever Read about Sleep*
- **Author:** Trudee Romanek
- **Grade Level:** 2–6
- **Summary:** This book shares fascinating information about sleep, including stages of sleep, circadian rhythms, the consequences of lack of sleep, what scientists say about dreaming and sleepwalking, and more.

### *Double-Entry Journal*

| **Interesting Information** | **Response** |
| --- | --- |
| *Tests show that when you stay up until 3 a.m., the next day your body has 30 percent fewer "natural killer cells"—the cells that fight viruses.* | *My parents have told me that I need sleep in order to fight illness. Now I believe them!* |
| *During Stage 4 [deep sleep], your body produces the largest amount of some of the chemicals that help you grow.* | *This is really interesting and important. If I want to grow taller, I need to be sure to get plenty of sleep.* |

EXAMPLE 3.21

- **Title:** *Locomotion*
- **Author:** Jacqueline Woodson
- **Grade Level:** 5–8
- **Summary:** Lonnie Collins Motion's life changes when his parents die in a fire and he and his sister are sent to separate foster homes. A teacher helps him express his feelings, memories, and hopes in free verse. As Lonnie notes in the beginning, the entire book is a poem because every time he tries to tell the whole story, his mind goes Be Quiet!

### *Double-Entry Journal*

| **Quote** | **Response** |
| --- | --- |
| *"Look at Little Brother Lonnie all growed up." (page 82)* | *Rodney's saying this makes me happy and warm because it shows that Lonnie was accepted by Rodney as a part of the family. What a great, great guy Rodney is. Lonnie's reaction made me feel even better, almost as if I were him. I was so happy I almost cried.* |
| *"You think it's still flying through the air somewhere?" (page 86)* | *Wow. This is a really different thought. I can picture a kiss you blow flying through the air. How sad that Lonnie wonders if his kiss ever made it to his parents the night they died. He wonders if it's just floating out there somewhere. I can't imagine having your parents die without warning and never getting to say good-bye. I'll never think of blown kisses in the same way.* |

Reading logs, or literature logs, are more directed than double-entry journals in that the teacher provides a prompt for writing following a period of sustained silent reading or a shared reading experience. Kelly and Farnan (1991) have argued that reading logs can be effective in promoting the critical thinking skills of analysis and evaluation and in promoting personal interactions with text if the appropriate prompts are provided. Appropriate prompts are those that elicit a reader's perception of, association with, or evaluation of the text. Kelly and Farnan have provided a list of 16 reader-response prompts, including the following: "What character was your favorite? Why?" "What character did you dislike? Why?" "Are you like any character in the story? Explain." "Does anything in this work remind you of your own life or something that happened to you?" "What was your first reaction to the story?" "If you were a teacher, would you read this book to your class?"

Each of these questions emphasizes the students' personal interpretations and interactions with the text. Non–reader-response prompts are those that focus exclusively on the text, such as "Tell me about your book." When the reader-response prompts were used with fourth-grade students, Kelly and Farnan found that students went beyond a literal response to the text and engaged in thinking that involved analysis of text from a variety of perspectives.

## EXAMPLE 3.22

- **Title:** *Criss Cross*
- **Author:** Lynne Rae Perkins
- **Grade Level:** 5–10
- **Summary:** This multigenre book shares realistic, often poignant, moments in the hearts and lives of several 14-year-olds growing up in a small town.

### *Reading Log*

**Prompt** (after reading Chapter 1): Find a sentence in this chapter that is particularly interesting or intriguing to you. What is your reaction to the sentence?

**Response:** *"At some point you just had to go change your clothes in a bush" (page 44). I thought this sentence was funny! I laughed aloud when I read it. Debbie and Patty were changing their clothes in a bush on their way to school because their mothers did not permit them to wear certain styles. I think lots of mothers are like this. The girls tried to convince their mothers that the current fashion was acceptable, but their mothers just didn't get it. Debbie and Patty concluded that eventually you just give up trying to convince your mothers and do what you want . . . even if it means changing clothes in a bush! LOL!*

---

Partner journals (sometimes referred to as dialogue journals) require students to interact with another person, often a classmate or a student at another school, perhaps in another state or country, who is reading the same book. The students may react to a chapter after it is read or the teacher may offer prompts. Partner journals stimulate purposeful communication, provide an opportunity for writing, and allow for feedback. Morgan and Albritton (1990) have reported success with this activity with children as young as second-graders and found that both the content and the form of student writing improved over time.

EXAMPLE **3.23**

- **Title:** *Kira-Kira*
- **Author:** Cynthia Kadohata
- **Grade Level:** 5–8
- **Summary:** This Newbery Medal winner portrays the prejudice, financial hardships, grueling work conditions, and devastating illness faced by a Japanese American family in the 1950s. In spite of these realities, the book conveys hope for the future.

### *Partner Journal*
#### *(After Chapter 7)*

*Dear Journal Partner:*

*Wow. This chapter was interesting. I felt so sorry for Katie. It would be horrible to have to wait in a hot car all day while your parents are working. I know my parents don't like to leave me home alone—although I could handle it—but I don't think they'd ever make me stay in a car all day. I guess Katie's parents didn't feel like they had a choice. Wouldn't you get out of the car and get some fresh air or stretch your legs? I would. It's a good thing her younger brother mostly slept. Can you imagine if he was fussy? It was sad how exhausted and worried their mother was when she came out for her lunch break, and I felt bad for her when she woke from her nap with a start and ran back into the factory.*

*Your Partner*

*Dear Partner:*

*It was unbelievable that a couple of kids would have to wait in a car all day long. HOW BORING. I think I might be a little scared, too. I felt bad about how exhausted Katie's mother was. My parents work really hard, too, and they don't have much time for me. I kind of resent it like Katie does, even though I know they're working hard for our family. Even so, I'd like to have their attention (most of the time!).*

*My parents are part of a union. I thought it was interesting that Katie's mom said that forming a union is wrong because it fights the people who are paying the workers. I don't agree. Remember when we were studying unions in history? Kind of a different perspective.*

*Your Partner*

Family members can be included in the journal experience also. If the family member has read the book, both he or she and the student can respond to the literature, sharing their points of view and their reactions. If the family member has not read the book, then he or she can respond to the student's comments by asking questions, requesting clarification, and reacting to the student's comments. In Example 3.24, a second-grade child read *Sea Turtles* in class, wrote in his partner journal, then took the book and the journal home to his parents. Both parents responded. The book and journal were returned to school several days later. The boy waited until he was at school to read his parents' responses.

Fuhler (1994) described an experience she had with her junior high students and their parents in which the parents were invited to read the same book as their children and to participate in a dialogue about the book through the use of a partner journal. She found that most parents were delighted to be involved in the activity, and she was impressed with the thoughtful responses made by both parents and students.

E X A M P L E  **3.24**

- **Title:** *Sea Turtles*
- **Author:** Gail Gibbons
- **Grade Level:** K–2
- **Summary:** The author describes the variety of sea turtles, discusses their habits, explains people's efforts to protect them, and compares them to land turtles. This book is rich in information and a useful resource for young readers.

### *Partner Journal*

*Dear Mom and Dad:*

*I like reading about sea turtles. They are my favorite animal. Did you know they live a long, long time? Can I see one sometime?*

*Dan*

*Dear Dan:*

*This was an interesting book! It is fascinating that sea turtles can live to be over 100 years old! I learned other things about sea turtles that I never knew. For instance, I didn't know that sea turtles have been around for millions of years. Wow! I also didn't know that they lay about 100 eggs at a time! Imagine a human mother having 100 babies!!*

*I hope we will see a sea turtle some time. Maybe we can go to the aquarium soon.*

*Love,*

*Dad*

*Hi Danny!*

*I had desert tortoises when I was young. They used to hibernate in the winter. We never knew quite where they went—one day we'd go outside and couldn't find them. Then, months later, they'd reappear! I learned from your book that sea turtles disappear too! They don't hibernate, but they do migrate—travel a long distance away—when they are going to have their young.*

*Share another book with me soon!*

*Love,*

*Mom*

When teachers respond to journals, it is important that they focus on the message and not the form of the students' writing. Teachers should limit correction of spelling, punctuation, and syntax (although they should use their observations of students' developing writing skills to inform instruction) while modeling standard usage as they respond in writing to the content of students' entries. Responses should be nonjudgmental, encouraging, and thought stretching (Fuhler, 1994; Hancock, 1993). An emphasis on students' ideas is particularly supportive of English learners because genuine and purposeful dialogue is promoted, a nonthreatening context for writing is established because the work is not "corrected," and teacher responses provide a model of effective writing and elaboration.

**English learners**

Journals provide readers with the opportunity to think about and share their feelings and thoughts about characters, events, and ideas throughout their reading of a book. They give students a voice in their reading, and allow them to collaborate with an author as they create meaning together (Fuhler, 1994). A variety of journal formats should be used throughout the course of a school year, because each type provides a different kind of experience for both the teacher and the student. Further, as we noted in Chapter One, journals provide an opportunity for differentiation as teachers vary the journal form and the prompts.

## Character Blogs

**Technology**

Blogs, short for web logs, are interactive websites that serve as online journals and can include photographs, videos, and links to other websites. Millions of people around the world have established blogs to communicate with others about a topic of interest, to chronicle their travels, and to share their personal musings. Blogs are increasingly being used in education because they provide students with an authentic audience and feedback for their ideas and writings.

Because blogs are produced with an active writer in mind and are designed to communicate an identity, a personality, and a point of view (Kennedy, 2003), they are an ideal environment for students to assume the voice of a character in a book they are reading and to recount the experiences, thoughts, and hopes of the character as they see them. Classmates and others are encouraged to respond to the log entries with questions and comments.

Character blogs help students connect with books and characters. When students step inside a character's mind and heart and write from the character's perspective, a high level of involvement and identification is attained (Hancock, 1993). Readers grow in their understanding of the actions, motives, and emotions of the character. Hancock found in working with her eighth-grade students that they also needed the opportunity to react from their own viewpoint, and so students should be permitted to respond to their own character entry with a personal comment if they choose. By thinking about both the character's perspective and their own, students may acquire insights into their own histories, values, and ideals, and thus gain a greater sense of their identities—adding a powerful dimension to this activity.

Example 3.25 shares sample entries and comments from a blog created by a student who is reading *The Red Rose Box* by Brenda Woods. She first writes to share her feelings about the gift she received from her mysterious Aunt Olivia. Classmates respond to the entry (which are typically viewed by clicking on "comments" but are shown here) and can continue to do so even after the writer posts her next entry. Note that the most recent entry is at the top of the page. Previous entries will appear in reverse chronological order beneath it.

If you wish to learn more about blogs, type "blogs in education" into your Internet search engine for a wealth of information, including sites for models and best practices. You will also want to check school and district policies regarding the use of blogs in the classroom. As a safety measure, students should not use their real names on blogs.

## EXAMPLE 3.25

- **Title:** *The Red Rose Box*
- **Author:** Brenda Woods
- **Grade Level:** 4–6
- **Summary:** Leah Jean and her sister Ruth live below the Mason-Dixon Line in rural Sulfur, Louisiana. Their lives take a dramatic turn when their parents are killed in a hurricane and they move in with their Aunt Olivia in Los Angeles, where wealth and freedom from segregation contrast sharply with their former lifestyle. The comforts of their new home, however, cannot substitute for the warm, loving family they lost in Louisiana.

### *Character Blog*

**Friday, September 24**

**No Worries!**

*Dear Friends,*

*Thanks for your concern, but my mom is not only letting me go, she and my sister Ruth and my Gramma are all going too! We borrowed travel cases from Sister Goodnight and mama is making Ruth and me new dresses. She said we are going to ride on a "Jim Crow" train and sit in the back until we cross a line and then we can sit anywhere. I'll write more about it later.*

*Leah Jean*

**Comments**

**No Worries!**

**#1   September 25 — 16:10**

*Hi Leah Jean. Have a good trip! Who is Sister Goodnight? Is that her real name? Tell me more about the Jim Crow train when you can, and be sure to post a picture of Los Angeles when you get there, if you can.*

*Your friend,*

*Guitar Guy*

**Wednesday, September 22**

**The Box**

*Hey Everyone! You are not going to believe it! I got a surprise birthday gift from my Aunt Olivia in California. My mom and she have not talked for years. (I don't know what's up with them because my mom won't tell me.) The coolest stuff was in the box, including jewelry, a real watch, a fancy bed jacket, and . . . train tickets to Los Angeles!! I'm so excited. You never know! Maybe I will be writing next from Los Angeles!*

*See ya,*

*Leah Jean*

**Comments**

**The Box**

**#1 September 22 — 17:05**

*Wow Leah. Sounds like a great surprise. No wonder you're excited. If your mom doesn't talk to her sister, do you really think she's going to let you go to California? Just wondering.*

*Dan the Man*

**#2 September 23 – 10:45**

*Hi Leah. I'm glad you're happy but I agree with Dan the Man. Don't get your heart set on going!*

*Soccer Girl*

# Feelings Charts

A feelings chart is useful in helping students analyze characters' reactions to one or more events in a literature selection. The chart also may serve as a vehicle for comparing and contrasting characters and is beneficial in building vocabulary.

The teacher prepares by identifying several events that occur in the literature and then listing the characters who are influenced by the event. Events are listed, as in Example 3.26, down the side of a chart. Characters are listed across the top of the chart. As the students read or listen to a selection, they are asked to provide a one-word description of each character's feelings at the time of each event. Their descriptions are written where the respective characters and the events intersect on the chart.

EXAMPLE **3.26**

- **Title:** *The Wave*
- **Author:** Margaret Hodges
- **Grade Level:** 2–3
- **Summary:** The people of a village in Japan are threatened by a destructive tidal wave. Only an old man who resides at the top of a hill sees the danger. He attempts to warn the villagers by burning his precious rice fields.

## Feelings Chart

| Events | Characters | | |
|---|---|---|---|
| | **Ojiisan** | **Tada** | **Villagers** |
| The water was calm and the village children played in the gentle waves. | *content* *satisfied* *happy* | *glad* *happy* *playful* | *thankful* *secure* *lucky* *peaceful* *cheerful* |
| Ojiisan sets fire to the rice fields. | *awful* *bad* *sad* *worried* | *anxious* *puzzled* *curious* *upset* *horrified* | *excited* *surprised* *unlucky* *vengeful* *angry* *crazy* |
| The huge tidal wave strikes the beach. | *afraid* *hopeful* *thankful* | *scared* *afraid* *panic* | *scared* *frightened* *terrified* *afraid* |
| The villagers, Ojisan, and Tada look down upon the empty beach where their village used to stand. | *successful* *relieved* *right* | *proud* *amazed* | *lucky* *thankful* *sad* *dazed* *forgiving* *grateful* *horrified* *amazed* *shocked* |

Students may develop charts in small groups or the teacher may facilitate the development of a whole-class chart.

Three student teachers modeled an interesting approach to this activity in a university seminar. The student teachers displayed the chart identifying key events in the story in the front of the room and then read the book aloud, pausing after each event. At each pause, they distributed small self-adhesive pieces of paper to everyone in the class and directed those students sitting on the right side of the classroom to write a single word that described how Ojiisan felt at the time. Students in the center of the classroom each wrote a word describing how

Tada felt, and those students on the left side of the classroom wrote a word describing the feelings of the villagers. Each member of the class was permitted to write only one word. Then students, one row at a time, were instructed to post their papers on the chart in the appropriate place. After all papers had been displayed, each contribution was read and discussed. The variety of words generated by the class was astounding, and the reaction from the students was one of interest and curiosity. The responses in Example 3.26 are a sampling of those given by the university students. Some students may wish to include a column labeled "Me" so they have an opportunity to respond to the events as well.

EXAMPLE 3.27

- **Poem:** "Casey at the Bat"
- **Book:** *The Family Book of Best Loved Poems* (David L. George, ed.)
- **Poet:** Ernest Lawrence Thayer
- **Grade Level:** 5 and up
- **Summary:** Fans count on Casey to win the baseball game. When he strikes out, it is a sad day in the history of Mudville.

### Feelings Chart

| Events | Characters | | |
| --- | --- | --- | --- |
| | **Casey** | **The Crowd** | **Me** |
| Casey steps up to bat. | | | |
| The umpire calls, "Strike Two!" | | | |
| Casey strikes out. | | | |

## Contrast Charts

Contrast charts are described in Chapter Two as a prereading activity. These charts are also useful during reading as a means for recording contrasting ideas or information in a selection as it is read. For example, students may list the pros and cons of an issue, the advantages and disadvantages of a course of action, or the two sides of an argument as they are described in the selection. After information from the selection has been organized in this manner, the chart may serve as a guide for writing. In Example 3.28, students record a character's reasons for and against taking a teddy bear to a sleepover while they are reading or listening to the story.

EXAMPLE $3.28$

- **Title:** *Ira Sleeps Over*
- **Author:** Bernard Waber
- **Grade Level:** K–3
- **Summary:** Ira has been invited to spend the night at a friend's house. He is very excited until his sister asks him whether he plans to take along his teddy bear. Ira wrestles with this question because he doesn't want to appear baby-ish to his friend, but he has never slept without "TaTa."

### Contrast Chart

| Reasons Why Ira Should Take His Teddy Bear | Reasons Why Ira Should Not Take His Teddy Bear |
| --- | --- |
| *He's never slept without it.* | *His friend will laugh at him.* |
| *They're going to tell scary stories.* | *He'll think Ira is a baby.* |
| *His friend's house is very dark.* | *His friend will laugh at the bear's name.* |

## Ten Important Words

The ten important words activity supports students' active engagement with text as they read to identify important words in a selection, compare their words to those selected by peers, and then write a one-sentence summary of the selection (Yopp & Yopp, 2003). First, each student is provided with a copy of a reading selection and a set of self-adhesive notes. The teacher instructs the students to independently identify the ten most important words in the text as they read—that is, the words that capture the most significant ideas in the selection—and record one word on each of ten self-adhesive notes. As the students silently read the selection, they choose and record words, revise their choices with continued reading, choose additional words, reread the selection, and make final decisions about word choices.

When each of the students has settled on a personal set of ten words, the teacher assists the students in building a group bar graph of the words and then leads a discussion about this visual display of the students' word choices. What patterns are seen? Which words were frequently selected by students? Why were some words selected by so many students? Which words are unique? Why might those words have been chosen by a member of the class? What does a particular word mean? Observations about the word selections stimulate discussion about the content of the text, and students elaborate on their word choices by explaining how the word is used in the text. After selecting ten important words from Gail Gibbons's *From Seed to Plant,* one student might volunteer, "I chose *wind* because the wind blows pollen from flower to flower, and this is what seeds need to grow." Another might say, "I chose *travel* because seeds sometimes travel far from the plant they grew on because they're carried away by birds or water or wind." Students are usually quite interested in the choices of their peers and often comment on why they did or did not choose the same word as others in the class, what they found most interesting in the text, and how they might reconsider their choices now that they have talked with their peers about the words and the reading selection.

After the discussion, each student writes a one-sentence summary of the text. Their own reading of the text, their selection of important words, and their discussion with peers support the students' efforts to summarize the text. Summaries usually reflect a deep understanding of the reading selection that results from the thoughtful interactions with the text and peers about the important ideas. Example 3.29 shares one student's ten important words and summary.

**English learners**

The emphasis on vocabulary and big ideas in the reading selection, the oral elaboration of ideas in the text as students discuss word choices, and the visual display of word selections support English learners in their efforts to negotiate meaning in the text and to use academic language to summarize the text.

Further, because student names are not written on the self-adhesive notes, participation is low risk and students feel comfortable contributing to the chart. Additional support can be provided by allowing students to select their ten important words with a partner in the first step of this activity if the material is challenging.

EXAMPLE **3.29**

- **Title:** *Spinning Spiders*
- **Author:** Melvin Berger
- **Grade Level:** K–3
- **Summary:** Many interesting facts about the variety of spider webs, the manner in which they are spun, and the purposes they serve are shared in this book.

### Ten Important Words

*spiders*

*spiderwebs*

*arachnids*

*spinnerets*

*different*

*threads*

*silk*

*sticky*

*prey*

*insects*

**Summary Sentence:** *Thousands of types of eight-legged arachnids use their spinnerets to make strong, sticky, silk thread that they weave into different kinds of webs to capture and wrap up their insect prey.*

In Example 3.30, students worked in pairs to select words, built a class graph, and then wrote summary statements with their partners. They did this at two points during their reading of *Harvesting Hope: The Story of Cesar Chavez* by Kathleen Krull, first as they read about Chavez's early life in the beginning of the book and later as they read about his protest years. Working their way through the text in this manner, the students built brief summaries that captured key ideas from the book. The work of one pair of students is shared in this example.

EXAMPLE 3.30

- **Title:** *Harvesting Hope: The Story of Cesar Chavez*
- **Author:** Kathleen Krull
- **Grade Level:** K–6
- **Summary:** In this Pura Belpré Honor Book, readers learn about Cesar Chavez's early years and his peaceful protest against the conditions of California farm workers.

## Ten Important Words
### (First Part of the Book)

Chavez

ranch

drought

landowners

school

farms

California

migrants

fields

powerless

**Summary Sentence:** *Chavez's family had to leave their ranch in Arizona after a drought and go to California where they became migrant workers and lived and worked in terrible conditions.*

## Ten Important Words
### (Second Part of the Book)

change

nonviolence

fight

La Causa

National Farm Workers Association

huelga

grapes

march

capitol

contract

**Summary Sentence:** *Chavez organized a huelga (strike) and a march to the state capitol to fight for change with talk, not violence.*

As a follow-up to this activity, the teacher might ask students to view related websites that he or she has previously identified and bookmarked. Students search for one or two of their important words on the websites to see whether and how the words are used, furthering their understanding of both the words and the content.

## CONCLUSION

During-reading activities enhance students' understanding of a text by prompting the use of comprehension strategies; facilitating thinking about ideas, text elements, or language; and promoting collaborative constructions of meaning. They also prompt personal responses to literature. During-reading activities engage students with a text, inviting them to think deeply about what they are reading and to share their thinking with peers.

### CHAPTER FOUR

# Postreading Activities

## Postreading

### Purposes

- To encourage personal responses
- To stimulate thinking
- To identify what is meaningful
- To promote reflection
- To facilitate organization, analysis, and synthesis
- To share and build interpretations
- To prompt connections

### Activities

- Polar opposites
- Literary report cards
- Character trait charts
- Plot profiles
- Powerful passages
- Sketch to stretch
- 3-D responses
- Multimedia responses
- Dramatic responses
- Venn diagrams
- Book charts
- Internet investigations

The postreading activities students engage in will have an impact on how they view the reading selection as well as the reading act. If students reflect on important ideas, share reactions, return to the book to achieve greater understanding, make connections with what they have read, engage thoughtfully with peers, and creatively respond to the literature, the selection will be viewed as a source of enjoyment and will be long remembered. Reading will be viewed as a meaningful and satisfying activity. If, on the other hand, students answer a series of low-level questions, work quietly, prove that they can sequence events by numbering them on a worksheet, and complete a crossword puzzle to reinforce vocabulary, then they are likely to view the selection as simply a vehicle for skills instruction. Reading will be perceived as an exercise.

The postreading activities we provide in this chapter are in keeping with the reasons for using literature in the classroom. In particular, they promote enjoyment of reading by encouraging personal responses to literature, stimulating thinking about ideas and issues in books, and inviting students to identify what is meaningful to them. They deepen students' understandings of the book by providing structures to help students reflect on the text; organize, analyze, and synthesize information and ideas; and share and build interpretations with peers. They promote extension of comprehension beyond the text as students make connections among books and with their own lives.

The first several activities—*polar opposites*, *literary report cards*, and *character trait charts*—provide students with a framework for reflecting on characters. They require analysis of characters' behaviors and language and the author's word choices in order to draw conclusions about characters. *Plot profiles* provide a graphic means for organizing and analyzing the plot of a story. *Powerful passages* prompt students to revisit the literature to identify a portion of the text that appeals to them. They search for interesting or powerful ideas, events, and language to share with peers. *Sketch to stretch*, *3-D responses*, *multimedia responses*, and *dramatic responses* invite students to respond creatively to a reading selection. *Venn diagrams* facilitate comparisons between two or more characters, settings, events, or books, or between a character and the readers themselves. *Book charts* are useful for examining several books by the same author, on the same topic, or with the same theme. *Internet investigations* move students beyond the book to the larger world in which it is embedded and allow them to extend their understandings of ideas contained in the book.

**Technology**

**Technology**

Thus, the postreading activities presented in this chapter may be used for the following purposes:

- To encourage personal responses
- To stimulate thinking about ideas and issues
- To invite students to identify what is meaningful to them
- To promote reflection on the text
- To facilitate organization, analysis, and synthesis of information and ideas
- To provide opportunities for sharing and building interpretations with peers
- To prompt connections among books and with students' lives

Students at all levels of reading development can participate meaningfully in the activities presented in this chapter. The activities promote higher-level thinking while also providing scaffolds for students' rich interactions with the literature. Several of the activities reduce linguistic demands by providing opportunities for nonlinguistic representations of understandings and responses. The activities invite diverse and creative responses that honor the reader.

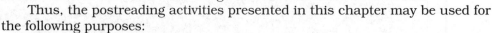

**English learners**

# Polar Opposites

The polar opposites activity provides a structure for students to analyze characters in a reading selection. Students rate characters on a variety of traits and draw examples from the text to support their ratings.

To develop a polar opposites guide, the teacher begins by selecting a character and generating a list of traits that describe him or her. Then the teacher identifies the opposite of each of those traits. For example, if a character is very sure of himself, has many friends, and is easily angered, the list might include "confident," "popular," and "hot-tempered." Opposites of these might be "unsure," "unpopular," and "easygoing." Opposites used will depend on the precise meaning intended by the initial term. Each pair of opposites makes up its own scale, as seen in the examples that follow. After reading a selection, students rate the character(s) by placing a mark on each scale.

Students may work individually to rate characters, or they may work in pairs or small groups and come to consensus. Alternatively, the teacher may provide a large chart in the classroom that displays several scales onto which students record their ratings with tally marks. In this way, student opinions are compiled in one place and students can see what the prevailing and minority opinions are at a glance.

In Example 4.1, we have placed an *X* on each scale to show possible student responses. Responses will vary.

## EXAMPLE 4.1

- **Poem:** "The Road Not Taken"
- **Book:** *You Come Too* (Robert Frost)
- **Poet:** Robert Frost
- **Grade Level:** 4 and up
- **Summary:** A traveler reflects on his decision to take a less traveled road.

### Polar Opposites

The traveler was

| | | | | | | |
|---|---|---|---|---|---|---|
| thoughtful | _X_ | ____ | ____ | ____ | ____ | impulsive |
| timid | ____ | ____ | ____ | _X_ | ____ | courageous |
| disappointed | ____ | ____ | ____ | _X_ | ____ | content |
| realistic | ____ | _X_ | ____ | ____ | ____ | unrealistic |
| a follower | ____ | ____ | ____ | ____ | _X_ | a leader |

Nowhere in the poem does the poet explicitly state that the traveler is thoughtful or impulsive, timid or courageous, disappointed or content, and so on. Students must examine the traveler's behaviors and thoughts in order to form judgments.

Students then discuss their ratings with classmates. It is during discussion that students give voice to their ideas and their mental processes become public.

Readers who may be having difficulty interpreting the text are exposed to the thinking of peers as reasons for ratings are shared and evidence from the text is cited. Further, students may be exposed to multiple perspectives and ways of thinking about the text. Any rating should be considered acceptable as long as students support their responses with information from the text or from their own knowledge or experiences.

When constructing polar opposites, the teacher decides how many points to include on the scale based on his or her knowledge of the students. A three-point scale is used in Example 4.2. *The Story of Ferdinand*, by Munro Leaf, is generally read with young children who may have difficulty making the finer discriminations required on scales with more points. In this example, students write responses or dictate them to an adult prior to or as they engage in discussion.

## EXAMPLE 4.2

- **Title:** *The Story of Ferdinand*
- **Author:** Munro Leaf
- **Grade Level:** K–1
- **Summary:** Ferdinand the bull is very different from other bulls. He is big and strong, but he is not interested in butting heads and fighting. He prefers to sit and smell flowers.

### Polar Opposites

Ferdinand is

happy  __X__  _____  _____  sad

*He seems to be very happy as long as he can sit and smell flowers. He was even happy in the bull's ring because he could smell the flowers in the ladies' hair.*

healthy  __X__  _____  _____  unhealthy

*He is big and strong, which means he must be healthy.*

fierce  _____  _____  __X__  tame

*Ferdinand likes to sit. He is not interested in fighting.*

same  _____  _____  __X__  different

*Ferdinand is different from other bulls. He is happy sitting, and the others like to fight and butt heads. He was not interested in being picked for the bull's ring. Other bulls tried hard to be picked.*

brave  __X__  _____  _____  fearful

*He must be fairly brave because he did what he wanted to do even though it was not like other bulls. Also, he did not seem upset about going into the bull's ring.*

## EXAMPLE 4.3

- **Title:** *The Watsons Go to Birmingham—1963*
- **Author:** Christopher Paul Curtis
- **Grade Level:** 5–8

■ **Summary:** In this humorous and deeply moving book, a black family from Michigan travels to Alabama during the height of the civil rights movement. The family encounters violence, and Byron, the oldest sibling, helps his brother recover from the wrenching experience of the bombing of a neighborhood church.

### *Polar Opposites*

Byron is

| | | | | | | |
|---|---|---|---|---|---|---|
| mean | ____ | ____ | ____ | ____ | ____ | kind |
| insensitive | ____ | ____ | ____ | ____ | ____ | sensitive |
| disrespectful | ____ | ____ | ____ | ____ | ____ | respectful |
| not likable | ____ | ____ | ____ | ____ | ____ | likable |
| unintelligent | ____ | ____ | ____ | ____ | ____ | intelligent |

A modification of the polar opposites activity is presented in Example 4.4. In *From the Mixed-Up Files of Mrs. Basil E. Frankweiler,* by E. L. Konigsburg, two characters have contrasting traits and may be rated on the same scales. Students write a "C" for Claudia and a "J" for Jamie at the appropriate point on each scale.

EXAMPLE 4.4

- ■ **Title:** *From the Mixed-Up Files of Mrs. Basil E. Frankweiler*
- ■ **Author:** E. L. Konigsburg
- ■ **Grade Level:** 5–6
- ■ **Summary:** Two children, Claudia and Jamie, run away from home and hide in a museum where they solve a mystery.

### *Polar Opposites*

| | | | | | | |
|---|---|---|---|---|---|---|
| tightwad | _J_ | ____ | ____ | ____ | _C_ | big spender |
| cautious | ____ | _C_ | ____ | _J_ | ____ | adventurous |
| predictable | ____ | _C_ | ____ | ____ | _J_ | spontaneous |
| messy | _J_ | ____ | ____ | ____ | _C_ | neat and tidy |
| organized | _C_ | ____ | ____ | ____ | _J_ | disorganized |

Polar opposites may be used successfully with all age groups to facilitate readers' reflections on characters. They offer a structure for discussions and encourage critical thinking as students analyze and synthesize what they know about a character in order to make judgments.

# Literary Report Cards

Literary report cards provide students with another format for reflecting on characters. In this activity, suggested by Johnson and Louis (1987), students issue grades to characters in a reading selection. Initially, the teacher selects the "subjects" on which the characters will be graded. Rather than academic areas, characters may be graded on personality traits, such as "courageous" or "patient." Eventually, the students generate the subject areas. Selection of subject areas requires higher-level thinking, as the students reflect on the character, analyze his or her qualities and behavior, and label the qualities. In addition to awarding the grades, students comment on or cite evidence for each grade. Report cards themselves may be modeled after report cards used at the school that the students attend.

EXAMPLE **4.5**

- **Title:** *Frindle*
- **Author:** Andrew Clements
- **Grade Level:** 3–5
- **Summary:** Nick is a creative fifth-grader who is known as a bit of a trouble-maker. He meets his match in Mrs. Granger, a strict language arts teacher who loves the dictionary. Nick causes much excitement with his invention of a new word—*frindle*—and gains national attention for the word and the trouble it causes at his school. Mrs. Granger is a great teacher and knows just what it takes to get students excited about words.

### Literary Report Card

| Student: Nicholas Allen | | |
|---|---|---|
| | *Grade* | *Comment* |
| Language arts | A | *Nick wrote an excellent, detailed report on the history of words. He has great presentation skills. He invented a new word.* |
| Creativity | A | *Nick turned a classroom into a tropical island. He has inventive ideas for postponing homework assignments.* |
| Leadership skills | A | *Nick persuaded his classmates to use the word frindle, even though they would get in trouble.* |
| Obedience | D | *Nick's new word caused problems at school. He didn't stop using the word when the teacher asked him to stop.* |
| Generosity | A | *Nick established a scholarship in Mrs. Granger's name.* |

EXAMPLE 4.6

- **Title:** *My Father's Dragon*
- **Author:** Ruth Stiles Gannett
- **Grade Level:** 2–4
- **Summary:** Elmer Elevator wishes to fly. When an alley cat tells him about a flying dragon that is being held captive on faraway Wild Island, Elmer runs away from home to rescue it. On the island, he meets many animals that try to interfere with his plans. He cleverly evades them all, frees the dragon, and they fly away together.

### *Literary Report Card*

**Airborne Elementary School**

Student: Elmer Elevator

| *Characteristic* | *Grade* | *Comment* |
|---|---|---|
| Kind | A | *Elmer befriends a cat and provides him with shelter and food.* |
| Adventurous | A | *Elmer wants to fly. He runs away to Wild Island.* |
| Obedient | D | *Elmer disobeys his mother. He runs away. He sneaks aboard a ship.* |
| Clever | A | *He is able to hide from the sailors. He finds a way to distract the animals on the island that try to eat him.* |
| Prepared | C | *Elmer takes a bag of supplies, but he doesn't carry enough food.* |

For primary-grade students, descriptors such as "good," "satisfactory," and "needs to improve" may be more appropriate than letter grades.

EXAMPLE 4.7

- **Title:** *The Tale of Peter Rabbit*
- **Author:** Beatrix Potter
- **Grade Level:** K–2
- **Summary:** Peter Rabbit disobeys his mother and goes to Mr. McGregor's garden. There he is chased by Mr. McGregor and barely escapes.

### Literary Report Card

|  | | |
|---|---|---|
| **O'Hare Private School** | | |
| Student: Peter | | |
| G—Good    S—Satisfactory    N—Needs to Improve | | |
| *Area* | *Grade* | *Comments* |
| Obedience | N | *He went to Mr. McGregor's garden even though his mother told him not to.* |
| Bravery | N | *He cried a lot when he got caught in a net and when he couldn't find his way out of the garden.* |
| Sports | G | *He ran fast, jumped into a bucket and out of a window, and wiggled under a fence.* |

Any grade given by the student should be accepted so long as he or she is able to provide a defensible reason for the grade. In Example 4.7, some students may give Peter Rabbit an "S" or a "G" in bravery rather than an "N," stating that he was brave to go into McGregor's garden. It is important that the teacher be open to a range of responses and focus on the students' abilities to provide reasonable, thoughtful explanations for the grades they award.

All graded areas should be stated in the positive form. It makes no sense to award a character an "A" in impatience, for example, or a "D" in dishonesty.

## Character Trait Charts

Character trait charts promote a thoughtful analysis of characters and also build students' vocabulary. In this strategy, described by Manyak (2007), students brainstorm words that describe what characters are "really like inside" after reading a text or portion of a text. As the teacher lists the terms on the board, students explain the reasons for their word choices, sharing incidents from the story that support their choices. Next, the teacher extends the students' thinking and language by sharing words that he or she preselected for use with the book. The teacher provides student-friendly definitions of the words, shares examples of their use, and asks whether the words apply to one or more of the characters in the book. Students discuss the word meanings, the story events, and complete a trait chart.

In Example 4.8, the teacher presented the students with several words after the students brainstormed their own descriptions of characters in *The Orange Shoes* (Noble, 2007). The teacher's list included *resourceful, appreciative, cruel, creative,* and *arrogant.* He asked the students to think about whether any of the characters is resourceful, or able to deal with difficult situations and make use of available resources to do so. The students readily noted that Delly is resourceful, explaining that she used old envelopes to create a sketch book. The teacher or students placed an *X* in the appropriate column on the chart. They then discussed other characters and determined that both the mother and the father also display the trait of resourcefulness—the mother because she made paint from natural materials in her environment and the father because he used old tire rubber to repair shoes. Some students argued that the teacher in the book is also resourceful, and so the appropriate notations were made. The classroom teacher then guided a discussion about each of the additional words and the students completed the chart as they reached consensus on the characters' traits.

Manyak (2007) argued that this strategy provides students with a rich context for thinking about new words to describe characters and suggested an interesting extension of the chart in which students explore character traits across stories. In Example 4.9, students listed the names of characters who display a given trait. Students identified both Lilly in *Julius the Baby of the World* and Prudy in *The Orange Shoes* as *jealous,* but they weren't comfortable with labeling them both as *cruel.* The chart remains posted in the room so students can add character names and traits as they read additional books.

## EXAMPLE 4.8

- **Title:** *The Orange Shoes*
- **Author:** Trinka Hakes Noble
- **Grade Level:** 1–4
- **Summary:** Buying new shoes for Delly stretches the family's finances, and when cruel classmates step on the beautiful shoes she proudly wears one day, Delly is devastated. However, she uses her artistic talent to creatively repair the damage, and she and her family enjoy and contribute to the Shoebox Social at her school.

### Character Trait Chart

|         | Resourceful | Appreciative | Cruel | Creative | Arrogant |
|---------|-------------|--------------|-------|----------|----------|
| Delly   | x           | x            |       | x        |          |
| Prudy   |             |              | x     |          | x        |
| Teacher | x           | x            |       |          |          |
| Father  | x           | x            |       |          |          |
| Mother  | x           | x            |       |          |          |

EXAMPLE 4.9

- **Titles:** *Julius the Baby of the World* (Kevin Henkes)
  *The Orange Shoes* (Trinka Hakes Noble)

### Character Trait Chart

| Jealous | Mischievous | Protective | Creative | Arrogant | Cruel |
|---------|-------------|------------|----------|----------|-------|
| Lilly   | Lilly       | Lilly      | Delly    | Prudy    | Prudy |
| Prudy   |             |            | Lilly    |          |       |
|         |             |            |          |          |       |
|         |             |            |          |          |       |
|         |             |            |          |          |       |

## Plot Profiles

In a plot profile (Johnson & Louis, 1987; see also DeGroff & Galda, 1992), students identify the main events in a story and then rate the events along some scale, such as level of excitement or impact on the character. Events are numbered, and these numbers are placed along a horizontal axis, as in Example 4.10. The rating for each event is plotted along the vertical axis. Lines are drawn between each point, thus creating a line graph. Johnson and Louis have suggested that when students rate events in terms of their excitement, they use the following scale: "Calm," "Very Interesting," "Exciting," "WOW!"

EXAMPLE 4.10

- **Title:** *Number the Stars*
- **Author:** Lois Lowry
- **Grade Level:** 4–6
- **Summary:** This is the story of one family's efforts to help save Danish Jews from the Nazis.

### Events

1. *Running home from school, Ellen, Annemarie, and Kirsti are stopped by German soldiers.*
2. *Peter visits after curfew and tells the family that Germans are ordering stores run by Jews closed.*
3. *Ellen comes to stay with the Johansens when her parents flee.*

4. *The soldiers search the Johansen apartment for the Rosen family. They challenge Ellen because of her dark hair.*
5. *Mrs. Johansen, Annemarie, Ellen, and Kirsti travel to Uncle Henrik's.*
6. *The girls play at Uncle Henrik's.*
7. *"Aunt Bertie's" loved ones gather around her casket.*
8. *The soldiers interrupt the gathering.*
9. *Peter organizes the Jews to head to the boat.*
10. *Mrs. Johansen leaves with the Rosens.*
11. *Annemarie sees her mother on the ground and helps her to the house.*
12. *Annemarie races through the woods to deliver the envelope to Henrik.*
13. *Annemarie is stopped and questioned by soldiers. They discover the package.*
14. *Uncle Henrik explains the Resistance and the handkerchief to Annemarie.*
15. *The war ends. Annemarie learns the truth about Lise's death.*

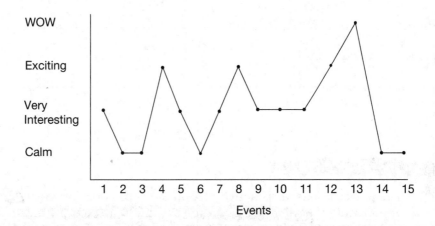

An alternative to a line graph is a cut-and-paste grid. Students write, and perhaps illustrate, key events from the story on separate pieces of paper. Students paste these events higher or lower on a large butcher paper grid, depending on the ratings they give. The key events and ratings shown in the line graph in Example 4.10 are depicted in the cut-and-paste format in Example 4.11. Students may work individually or collaboratively in small groups on plot profiles, coming to consensus on story events and ratings. If other individuals or groups of students are reading the same book, plot profiles may be compared. Teachers should expect differences between individual or group selections of key events and ratings.

EXAMPLE 4.11

| | | | Annemarie is stopped and questioned by soldiers. They discover the package. | | |
|---|---|---|---|---|---|
| **WOW** | | | | | |
| **Exciting** | | | | | |
| **Interesting** | Running home from school, Ellen, Annemarie, and Kirsti are stopped by German soldiers. | | | | |
| **Calm** | | Peter visits after curfew and tells the family that Germans are ordering stores run by Jews closed. | | Uncle Henrik explains the Resistance and the handkerchief to Annemarie. | The war ends. Annemarie learns the truth about Lise's death. |
| | 1 | 2 | 13 | 14 | 15 |

Events

# Powerful Passages

The powerful passages activity (Yopp & Yopp, 2003) provides students with the opportunity to identify in a reading selection an excerpt that they find compelling, interesting, or in some way personally meaningful and to share it with their peers. After reading a text, each student revisits the literature and skims it for a short passage he or she wishes to share. There are, of course, no "correct," "incorrect," "good," or "poor" choices. Selections are a matter of personal appeal. After each student has made a selection, students spend a few minutes quietly rehearsing their passages in preparation for reading aloud. Then students meet in pairs, read their passages to one another, and discuss the reasons for their choices. Students are given several opportunities to share their passages with different peers and, in turn, to listen to several peers' selections.

If everyone has read the same text, this activity provides a means for students to reexperience portions of the book together. Social interactions about passages enrich students' reflections on and responses to the book. Students notice commonalities and differences in their choices and gain insights into the thinking of their peers. Comprehension deepens as they listen and as they explain their reasons for and responses to their selection. Students' responses and explanations are often increasingly elaborated and sometimes revised as they share with additional partners.

This activity may also be used when students have read different texts, such as those read during a silent sustained reading period. Students select a passage from their respective books to share, rehearse it briefly, and then read it aloud to several different partners. Because students have a choice in what they share, the passages are discussed with personal commitment and enthusiasm, even passion. This enthusiasm can ignite the listeners' interest in the book.

The opportunity for rehearsal is particularly important for lower-achieving readers because it increases the likelihood of fluent oral reading. With rehearsal, reading aloud to peers is a successful and positive experience rather than an uncomfortable one, and this contributes to students' sense of competence.

An alternative to the oral sharing of passages is a written sharing. Participants select a passage to share and type and print it or copy it onto a piece of paper. These papers are then displayed around the classroom; the room becomes a gallery of powerful passages. The teacher and students circulate around the room to read the passages, carrying pencils so that they can write a response on any of the papers. Responses may be brief or lengthy and often take the form of comments such as "Oh, yes! I really enjoyed this part, too!" "I felt so bad when I read this part," "This was very funny! I like how the author spelled the words in the section to exaggerate the sounds," "Many of us selected this same passage!" "This really makes you think about how lucky you are and how much we don't know about other people in the world," "I was stunned when I read this section. It came so suddenly and was so unexpected. The book seemed so lighthearted at first, then changed with a few words." After the gallery walk, the group discusses the experience.

A variation on this open-choice activity is to ask students to peruse the text to locate passages of a particular type. Teachers may wish to have students

return to the text to find a passage that conveys emotion, provides information about the setting or a character, or clarifies a concept. A more focused discussion of the author's language can then occur.

Occasionally teachers ask students to select a single sentence rather than a passage. Students share their "significant sentences" in the same way as described for the powerful passages activity.

## Sketch to Stretch

Sketch to stretch offers readers an opportunity to think about and share what a text means to them as they recast their understandings from one symbol system, text, into a different symbol system, a sketch (Harste, Short, & Burke, 1988; Short, Kauffman, & Kahn, 2000; Whitin, 2002). By asking students to represent linguistic understandings in a nonlinguistic manner, teachers support students in thinking about, making connections to, elaborating on, and interpreting text. In addition, readers become more aware of whether they understand a text; comprehension monitoring is facilitated.

In sketch to stretch, students first listen to or read a text or portion of a text. The teacher then prompts them to sketch what the text means to them. They are encouraged to share through lines, colors, shapes, and pictures what they understand or feel about the ideas in the text. They show their sketches to small groups of peers who offer interpretations. After listening to the interpretations of peers, each artist explains his or her sketch. According to Whitin (2002), the sharing and explaining of the sketches provides students with an opportunity to revisit the text through literary discussions and to appreciate diverse perspectives of a text.

Although some students will sketch in silence, Whitin (2002) recommended that the students be permitted to talk to one another as they sketch if they choose. In her experience, students build on each other's ideas about a text as they sketch and come to understand that by collaborating they can construct meaningful interpretations and extend their ideas.

In Example 4.12, two fifth-grade students responded to *Grandfather's Journey* by Allen Say. One student shared that her sketch shows that Grandfather is in two places. "There is the ocean and the big farm field on one side, which is California, and on the other side, there are mountains, which is Japan. The line down the middle shows that he is in two places." The second student drew a picture that shows that Grandfather's heart is divided between his two countries.

## EXAMPLE 4.12

- **Title:** *Grandfather's Journey*
- **Author:** Allen Say
- **Grade Level:** K–6
- **Summary:** A Japanese American man tells the story of his grandfather's move to America and of his feelings of love and longing for both his native country and his adopted country.

## Sample Sketches

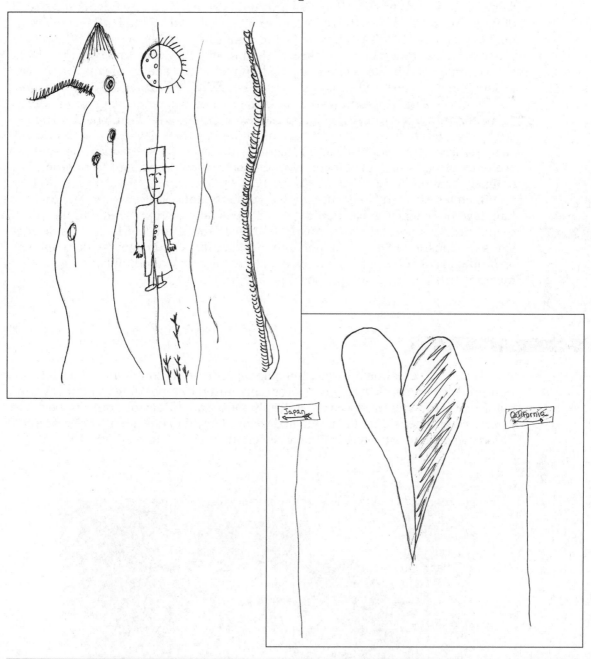

Short, Kauffman, and Kahn (2000) noted that sketch to stretch not only supports responses to a text as a whole but can also be used to help students think about a particular issue in a text. For example, if students want to discuss how Grandfather felt when he first saw the desert rock formations, farm fields, mountains, and rivers of the New World, they might create sketches that capture those feelings.

Although intended for use with students who have read or listened to the same book, sketch to stretch is also a valuable activity when students have read different texts. After a sustained silent reading time, for example, the teacher might ask students to sketch what the text they are reading means to them at this moment in time. Students sketch, then meet with peers who consider the sketch and generate ideas about the text and what the sketch means. Then the artist shares the text and explains the sketch. Students articulate their reasons for symbols, colors, lines, and so forth in their sketches, and they have an authentic reason to provide a brief summary of their reading selections. Further, students' interest in a peer's text may be piqued as they view the sketch and engage in discussion. Such social interactions about books are motivating, and students place "a high priority on reading books they hear about from others" (Palmer, Codling, & Gambrell, 1994, p. 177).

**English learners**

Sketch to stretch is effectively used with students of diverse reading and language proficiency levels. Sophisticated ideas may be represented in the students' sketches that otherwise might not be communicated verbally. The discussions that ensue provide an opportunity for language and cognitive development as students converse with one another, clarifying and extending language and meaning in a personal and purposeful communicative context.

## 3-D Responses

Like sketching, creating a three-dimensional representation of a reading selection provides students with a nonverbal medium for responding to literature and challenges students to process text deeply. Subsequent discussions support and extend comprehension and language development. When students are reading different books, their interest in new selections may be sparked.

Many materials can be manipulated and shaped into 3-D representations, including clay, playdough, straws, and pipe cleaners. One of our favorite materials is foil. After reading, students are provided a foil sheet of approximately 12 × 12 inches and asked to create a sculpture that captures an idea, feeling, event, character, or key point in the recently read selection. Students bend, twist, and tear the foil to serve their needs. This creative process may take anywhere from three to fifteen minutes.

After students have completed their foil creations, they turn to one or two neighbors to share. Classmates may be asked what they see in the work before the sculptor shares his or her thinking, or the sculptor of the piece may explain it immediately. Questions, clarifications, and elaborations are encouraged. Next, students may circulate around the classroom to examine all the foil creations, stopping and talking with one another as they circulate. Students are often intrigued by their peers' representations, and when all students have read the same book, they gain an appreciation for the variety of personal responses to a text.

**English learners**

The hands-on nature of this activity supports English learners in particular because a nonverbal medium is used to communicate responses to a reading selection, and students listen and speak to peers about their creations in pairs or small groups. The physical product provides an additional source of input and a context for language as students point to, manipulate, and use their creations in their conversations.

## Multimedia Responses

**Technology**

Multimedia responses allow students to creatively respond to a reading selection by utilizing a variety of technologies and resources. As the name indicates, multimedia responses include a combination of text, audio, still images, video, and animation. Students may use presentation software, such as Microsoft Power-Point or Apple Keynote, to construct their responses and import images and audio into a slide show. Or they may use a multimedia authoring tool or a digital video editor.

Multimedia responses promote conversations about works of literature and provide rich opportunities for meaning making and group problem solving. Sometimes, the teacher simply asks students to produce a response that is meaningful to them, inviting them to explore their own interests. On other occasions, he or she provides direction and differentiates the task so that students who need opportunities—for example, to continue to build their understanding of the academic vocabulary in an informational text—are asked to focus on important words, and those who are ready to think more deeply about the content are challenged to focus on key ideas and their application in novel situations. Students who need opportunities to think about character development in a narrative are asked to share events and dialogue from the selection that reveal character traits or that provide evidence of how the character changes over the course of the book. Students who would benefit from opportunities to think more abstractly or creatively are asked to develop a sequel to the book or to integrate a new character (such as a historical figure or character from another book) into the story line.

After the students decide on or are given a task, they brainstorm ideas and begin to organize them, perhaps using software such as Kidspiration or Inspiration to support their thinking. They develop their ideas and conduct research as needed. They might then create a storyboard, a graphic organizer that helps them map out and visualize their responses and experiment with changes before moving into the production phase of their work. Some teachers like to assign and review students' storyboards to ensure they are progressing well.

Next, after students have planned their responses, they develop the various multimedia elements. They draft text and download clip art and animation. They find still images to scan and import, locate images on the Internet, or use digital cameras to take pictures to include in their presentation. Also, students may audiotape sound effects, narration, or music. They use video cameras to film scenes or interviews. Multimedia responses allow students to express their ideas in multiple and rich ways and to tap the technological expertise of peers as they experiment with new tools and put the pieces of their response together. Students who may not be strong in other areas may have the opportunity to share technical skills and serve as a resource to classmates.

The last phase of the production is to put the elements together into a finished product and to review and refine or debug it as necessary. Finally, the students share their responses with classmates or with larger audiences by posting their work to the class web page or by burning their work on a DVD or CD and making it available in a class library.

Multimedia responses can take several days for students to complete but they are well worth the time. Indeed, Ivers and Barron (2006, p. 34) argued that the development of multimedia programs "can improve students' creativity and attitudes and promote a deeper and more sophisticated understanding of the content." We agree that the computer and other technologies offer students an important means to explore and revise their thinking and to share their responses to books in powerful ways.

Example 4.13 shares the first several slides of one third-grade group's PowerPoint response to *The Whingdingdilly* by Bill Peet. These students decided to explore and share the ways that dogs are special. They gathered information from various sources, including the Internet, and they interviewed classmates. The group made decisions about how to organize and present the information, and students divided the various production tasks among the group members.

E X A M P L E   **4.13**

- **Title:** *The Whingdingdilly*
- **Author:** Bill Peet
- **Grade Level:** 3–4
- **Summary:** Scamp, a farm dog, is unhappy that he is not as special as the award-winning horse at a neighboring farm. In an act of kindness, a witch transforms Scamp into a unique combination of animals. She calls the odd mix of camel, zebra, elephant, and other creatures a whingdingdilly. Scamp soon learns that his owner loved him just as he was, and he longs to be a dog again. Fortunately, the witch returns him to his original form.

***Multimedia Response***

| | |
|---|---|
| **What's So Special about Dogs?**<br><br>By<br>Amir, Sammy, & Shannon | *The Whingdingdilly* by Bill Peet is the story of a dog who doesn't think he's special, but . . . |

. . . dogs make great pets!

Here's why!
(Click on the links!)

- Dogs can do <u>tricks</u>.
- Dogs <u>play</u> with you.
- Dogs are <u>loyal</u>.

# *Dramatic Responses*

Students can engage in dramatic responses during or after reading a work of literature. Wilhelm (2002) uses the term *enactment* to describe dramatic responses to literature or units of study and explains that enactments involve students in depicting characters, actions, or ideas and interacting with each other in these roles. He argues that enactments make reading a transformative experience: Students begin to view themselves and the world in new ways as they think deeply about a text. Dramatic responses help students visualize what they read, assume various perspectives, connect to and elaborate on a text, negotiate and reflect on meaning, grow in their ability to interpret text, and pursue answers to questions raised by the text (Beach et al., 2006). Dramatic responses capitalize on the social nature of learning as students work together to re-create, explain, or extend a scene or an idea, and they motivate students to read, reread, and reflect on a book.

Perhaps the most obvious form of dramatic response is the creation of a play based on a book or portion of a book. Students work in small groups to identify important events in a story, for example, and decide how to re-create those events. They discuss and debate the content of their scene, assign roles, and plan their performance. The performers consider their selected character's appearance, actions, and motives. They think about the setting and the mood of the scene. They work with each other to prepare and then present their interpretation of the story. Sometimes, students produce a missing scene, one that might have occurred among several characters, or they incorporate shadow characters who explain how a character really feels or what he is really thinking after the character speaks. Students may choose to perform their scene live or to videotape it and share a recorded version with their classmates.

**Technology**

Alternatively, students may respond to a reading by creating a *tableau vivant*. Unlike a live action play, a *tableau vivant* (from the French meaning "living picture") is a frozen scene that captures a moment or idea in a book. Students identify a significant event or concept in a selection and work with peers to represent it with their bodies, creating a statue. After reading *The Wednesday Wars* by Gary D. Schmidt, for example, students select a key event and create a *tableau vivant* to depict the event. One group might choose the scene in which Mickey Mantle refuses to sign Holling Hoodhood's baseball. A startled and embarrassed Holling might look in shock at his ball, which has been tossed to the floor, while his friend Danny leans over a table to return his own signed ball to Mickey Mantle as a show of support for his friend and disgust for Mr. Mantle's behavior. Other students play Mickey Mantle and Mr. Baker, the owner of the Emporium where the famous baseball player made an appearance to sign baseballs. This is a powerful moment in the book, and the reader gains insight into both Holling and Danny's characters and wonders about the author's depiction of Mickey Mantle. Curious students may search the Internet to learn more about Mickey Mantle and his relationship with his fans and then share this

**Technology**

information with classmates.

Another group of students might select the moving scene in which Mrs. Bigio, an anguished and hostile school cafeteria worker whose husband dies in the Vietnam War, tells young Vietnamese refugee Mai Thi that she doesn't deserve to be comfortable and safe while American boys are suffering overseas. Students discuss the feelings and behaviors of Mrs. Bigio, Mai Thi, Holling, and other students present in the classroom as they decide on their pose.

Students can also create a *tableau vivant* to convey information from a work of nonfiction. After reading *The Story of Salt* by Mark Kurlansky, for example, students talk about the major ideas in the book and then plan and strike a pose that depicts an important idea. One group might portray salt's role in food preservation by posing as salt protecting food from bacteria. Another group might show salt's importance to international trade and power by representing countries making trade offerings for salt. A third group might pose as participants in Gandhi's Salt March.

Classmates can try to interpret each *tableau vivant*, or the students can explain their pose after sharing it with the class. Sometimes the students might present a series of poses as a narrator describes what is happening in each scene. Or students might, one at a time, step out of their pose while their peers remain frozen to share what they are thinking and feeling at this moment in the book. Teachers can take photographs of the *tableaux vivant* and post them on a

**Technology**

class website or use them as prompts for student writing.

Another format for dramatic response is a talk radio show. Students assume the roles of characters and respond to listeners who call in with questions or comments. Listeners might be other characters in the book, characters from different books, or the general public. What might the prince want to ask Elizabeth in Robert Munsch's *The Paper Bag Princess*, for example? What might the dragon say to Elizabeth? How might Cinderella (who is not a character in *The Paper Bag Princess* but is a well-known princess) interact with Elizabeth? What might the students themselves have to say to Elizabeth? Students think deeply about their characters and the characters with whom they speak as they pose and answer questions. They experience the lives of the characters and go beyond the words in the book to create the worlds in which the characters live.

In addition to plays, *tableaux vivant*, and talk radio shows are special report news broadcasts. Students consider an event, a character, or an idea from a book and generate a special report to inform the public about the topic. What

Technology

might a news reporter say about the launching of the *Merrimac*, the ironclad Civil War ship considered by many an "iron coffin" in *Iron Thunder* by Avi? Whom might the reporter interview? Someone aboard the ship? The builder? A skeptic? What events might the reporter select to share? Students might intersperse the live commentary with videotaped sequences, either of their own creation or downloaded from the Internet.

Dramatic responses provide students with an opportunity to examine the characters and ideas in books and then to become them. They deepen students' transactions with books and promote aesthetic responses to the literature. Furthermore, they allow for a rich diversity of responses and are appropriate for the full range of learners in a classroom.

## Venn Diagrams

Venn diagrams, named for the nineteenth-century British logician John Venn, offer a means for students to compare and contrast two or more characters, settings, or other information in a work of literature. Venn diagrams provide graphic representations, in the form of overlapping circles, of features that are unique and common to selected topics. The readers draw two or more overlapping circles and label each circle. Where the circles overlap, features common to the topics are listed, and where they do not overlap, features unique to each topic are recorded. Example 4.14 displays a Venn diagram comparing and contrasting fruit bats and birds from the book *Stellaluna*, by Janell Cannon.

EXAMPLE 4.14

- **Title:** *Stellaluna*
- **Author:** Janell Cannon
- **Grade Level:** K–3
- **Summary:** A fruit bat is cared for by a family of birds after falling from its mother's grasp while fleeing an owl. The bat and birds find that even though they are different, they are alike.

### Venn Diagram

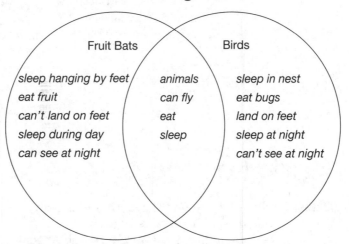

| Fruit Bats | animals | Birds |
|---|---|---|
| sleep hanging by feet | can fly | sleep in nest |
| eat fruit | eat | eat bugs |
| can't land on feet | sleep | land on feet |
| sleep during day | | sleep at night |
| can see at night | | can't see at night |

Comparisions can also be made across books, thus moving the students beyond "local reading" (Wolf in Hartman & Hartman, 1993)—a focus on individual works of literature with little or no effort to make connections across texts. For instance, the perspectives and actions of Johnny in *Johnny Tremain* by Esther Forbes can be compared and contrasted with those of Tim in *My Brother Sam Is Dead* by James Lincoln Collier and Christopher Collier. Each of these characters is a boy who lives during the time of the American Revolution. The lives and works of Sojourner Truth and Cesar Chavez can be examined in Example 4.15, and similarities and differences in *Adam of the Road* by Elizabeth Janet Gray, *The Door in the Wall* by Marguerite de Angeli, and *Crispin: The Cross of Lead* by Avi can be explored through the Venn diagram shown in Example 4.16.

EXAMPLE  4.15

- **Titles:**  *Only Passing Through: The Story of Sojourner Truth* (Anne Rockwell)
  *Harvesting Hope: The Story of Cesar Chavez* (Kathleen Krull)

- **Grade Level:**  K–6

- **Summaries:**  Each of these books describes an individual who became a champion of justice. Sojourner Truth was a slave who gained her freedom and traveled around the countryside to spread the truth about the conditions of slaves. Cesar Chavez, a migrant worker, organized peaceful protests and improved the lives of thousands.

### Venn Diagram

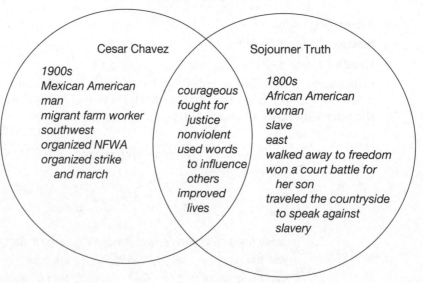

EXAMPLE  4.16

- **Titles:**  *Adam of the Road* (Elizabeth Janet Gray)
  *Crispin: The Cross of Lead* (Avi)
  *The Door in the Wall* (Marguerite de Angeli)

■ **Grade Level:** 5–8

■ **Summary:** Each of these books details the experiences of a boy growing up during the Middle Ages.

### Venn Diagram

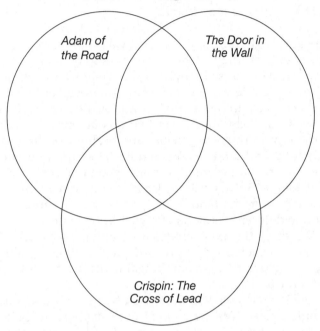

Adam of the Road

The Door in the Wall

Crispin: The Cross of Lead

## Book Charts

Book charts provide another structure for students to make connections across books. Through the use of book charts, students can discover patterns in literature, identify conventions in various genres, deepen and extend understandings of issues or concepts, and come to recognize the universality of certain themes. Students can compare and contrast characters' experiences and their responses to those experiences and analyze similarities and differences in plots. Through this activity, students' roles as readers are expanded beyond "the boundaries of a single text" (Hartman & Hartman, 1993, p. 202).

If all students in a class or group have read or listened to several of the same books, together they may develop a large chart on butcher paper that captures information from the books in a number of categories. If small groups of students have read different books that focus on the same topic or have a similar theme, then each group may contribute information about its book to a class chart. The teacher or students may prefer to create electronic versions of the chart that can be saved and updated.

**Technology**

A book chart that focuses on "the immigrant experience" may be developed when students have read *In the Year of the Boar and Jackie Robinson* by Bette Lord, *Dragonwings* by Laurence Yep, and *Journey to America* by Sonia Levitin. Categories on the chart may include book title, author, character, native country, positive experiences, and negative or challenging experiences.

"Survival" could be the focus of a book chart if students have read *The Sign of the Beaver* by Elizabeth George Speare, *Island of the Blue Dolphins* by Scott O'Dell, *Hatchet* by Gary Paulsen, and *Julie of the Wolves* by Jean Craighead George. In each of these books, the protagonist is stranded alone and must demonstrate resourcefulness and courage in order to survive. Categories for this book chart may include author, title, circumstances, internal challenges, external challenges, and outcome.

*Sylvester and the Magic Pebble* by William Steig, *The Magic Fish* by Freya Littledale, and *The Three Wishes* by M. Jean Craig each have a character in the story who is granted wishes. Students may record the title, author, wishes made, and the consequences of the wishes for each of these books. Students may also include wishes they would make given the opportunity. Thus, book charts can prompt both efferent and aesthetic responses.

Western (1980) has described a book chart in which students compare the characters, settings, problems, and endings of three versions of "Jack and the Beanstalk" and analyze their similarities and differences. Many familiar stories have cultural variations that make good choices for book charts. *The Egyptian Cinderella* by Shirley Climo, *Moss Gown* by William Hooks, and *Yeh-Shen: A Cinderella Story from China* by Ai-Ling Louie are three books that allow students to examine different versions of a well-known story.

We share two book charts in Examples 4.17 and 4.18. On any book chart, a column in which students record their feelings, reactions, or book ratings also may be included. This column will invite students to share their responses to the literature.

Book charts may be developed by individuals, small groups of students, or the entire class. Teachers of younger students will likely play a greater role in facilitating classroom discussions and in recording information.

EXAMPLE **4.17**

■ **Focus:** Name and Identity

### Book Chart

| Title | Author | Grade Level | Protagonist(s) | Threat to Identity | Resolution |
|---|---|---|---|---|---|
| My Name Is Maria Isabel | Alma Flor Ada | 3–4 | Maria Isabel | Her teacher calls her Mary because there are two Marias in the class already. | Maria uses a writing assignment to express her greatest wish: to be called by her own name. The teacher does so. |
| When My Name was Keoko | Linda Sue Park | 4–6 | Sun-hee Tae-yul | The Japanese who occupy South Korea demand that Koreans take on Japanese names. | Sun-hee, Tae-yul, and their family keep their heritage alive in their hearts. The war ends and Korea is freed. |

| Title | Author | Grade Level | Protagonist(s) | Threat to Identity | Resolution |
|-------|--------|-------------|----------------|--------------------|------------|
| *My Name Is Yoon* | Helen Recorvits | 1–3 | Yoon | *A Korean immigrant to the U.S. is asked to write her name using the alphabet rather than the characters with which she is familiar.* | *Yoon recognizes that however her name is written, she is still Yoon.* |
| *The Name Jar* | Yangsook Choi | 1–3 | Unhei | *A new immigrant to the U.S. is worried that classmates will tease her about her Korean name. She considers suggestions for an American name.* | *Unhei decides to to keep her own name.* |

## EXAMPLE 4.18

- **Focus:** Overcoming Loss
- **Grade Level:** 4–8

### Book Chart

| Title | Author | Summary | The Loss | Dealing with the Loss |
|-------|--------|---------|----------|----------------------|
| *Love That Dog* | Sharon Creech | *With the encouragement of his teacher, a boy uses poetry to express his feelings about the death of his dog.* | *Dog* | *Through writing poetry* |
| *Out of the Dust* | Karen Hesse | *Billie Jo's mother and baby brother die tragically, and Billie Jo's hands are scarred by fire.* | *Mother, baby brother, and use of hands* | *By living one day at a time and by forgiving her father and herself* |
| *Locomotion* | Jacqueline Woodson | *Lonnie Collins Motion's life changes when his parents die in a fire and he and his sister are sent to separate foster homes. A teacher helps him express his feelings and memories in free verse.* | *Parents and sister* | *Through writing poetry* |

Another type of book chart is the inquiry chart, or I-chart (Hoffman, 1992). As can be seen in Example 4.19, students record questions they have about a topic and anything they already know related to the questions. Then the students consult a variety of sources and record their findings on the chart. At the bottom of the chart, students summarize information. Students must compare information across texts and sometimes reconcile conflicting data in order to complete their summaries.

EXAMPLE **4.19**

■ **Grade Level:** 2–4

### I-Chart

| Topic:<br><br>Frogs | What Is Their Habitat? | What Do They Eat? | What Preys on Them? | Other Interesting Facts | New Questions |
|---|---|---|---|---|---|
| What we know | | | | | |
| *It's a Frog's Life* (Steve Parker) | | | | | |
| *Very First Things to Know about Frogs* (Patricia Grossman) | | | | | |
| *The Frog* (Paul Starosta) | | | | | |
| *Frogs* (Gail Gibbons) | | | | | |
| Summary | | | | | |

**English learners**    It has been argued that opportunities for narrow reading—reading several texts by the same author or on the same topic—benefit English learners (Krashen, 2004; Peregoy & Boyle, 2009; Schmitt & Carter, 2000). An author's distinctive style, word and phrasing choices, and use of certain expressions become familiar to readers, and so reading the second or third book by an author is easier than reading the first. Similarly, books on the same topic have overlapping vocabulary, concepts, and structures. Each book read on a topic supports the comprehensibility of the next. The more familiar students are with the language and the content of a topic, the more easily students can read books on the topic. Book charts and I-charts offer students the opportunity for narrow reading.

Low-achieving readers experience the same advantages when reading multiple books by the same author or on the same topic. Their successful comprehension of texts will serve to motivate additional reading, which, in turn, supports reading development. Although it is important to read widely, jumping from one genre to another, one topic to another, or one discourse style to another with little opportunity for extended reading on the same topic or in the same genre gives low-achieving readers little chance to build comfort and competence with text. Exposure to the same concepts phrased or elaborated on differently across texts and repetition of key vocabulary across texts builds students' background knowledge and language, enabling them to have more successful interactions with text.

## Internet Investigations

Internet investigations enrich students' understandings of a book by engaging them in research about real events, people, places, or other information related to the book. Both fiction and nonfiction literature can prompt questions, and Internet investigations provide students with the opportunity to seek answers to those questions. During or after reading *Al Capone Does My Shirts* by Gennifer Choldenko, for example, students may want to know more about Al Capone—what crimes he committed, why he turned to a life of crime, when and how he died. An Internet search will yield a wealth of information about the man, enhancing students' understanding of and appreciation for the story. Likewise, students may want to know more about Alcatraz—its history, the geography of the area, and the infamous people who were imprisoned on the island. They may wonder about the guards and families that were housed on the island. Or, students may want to learn about autism and how it is treated today. This activity allows students to pursue the answers to their questions and to gather information of interest to them. Some students may not spontaneously generate questions during their reading. This activity nudges them to think about the book as a springboard for investigations, and listening to the questions of their peers can both promote curiosity about the book's content and help them develop their own questions.

The teacher begins by inviting students to share their questions about the book, either in small groups or as a whole class. Then the students generate a list of search terms they might use to find information related to their questions. Students select the topics of greatest interest to them and work independently or in teams searching the Internet and recording information related to their topics. Teachers of younger students might anticipate questions and identify appropriate websites, perhaps bookmarking them on a class computer so students can successfully navigate the Web to find relevant information. At the conclusion of the activity, students share what they learned.

In the first example, a student wonders about the setting of the book *Elijah of Buxton* by Christopher Paul Curtis. He records his questions and two search terms he will use to find information about the town. He identifies the websites on which he found pertinent information and shares his findings. Other students might want to learn more about the Underground Railroad or to investigate whether Frederick Douglass actually visited Buxton, as described in the story. The second example shares a student's search related to the topic of falconry, discussed briefly in *Good Masters! Sweet Ladies!* by Laura Amy Schlitz. The student's understanding of the book is enriched by her new insights about the history and sport of falconry.

## EXAMPLE 4.20

- **Title:** *Elijah of Buxton*
- **Author:** Christopher Paul Curtis
- **Grade Level:** 5–8
- **Summary:** Elijah lives with his parents and other freed and runaway slaves in Buxton, Canada, a settlement at the end of the Underground Railroad. He is the first child to be born free in the settlement, and this is the story of his adventures, including his journey into the United States to help a friend and his encounters with the horrors of slavery.

### Internet Investigation

| |
|---|
| **Questions:** *Is Buxton a real place? What was it like? Does it still exist today?* |
| **Search Terms:** *Buxton, Reverend William King* |
| **Internet Sites:** *www.buxtonmuseum.com*<br>*http://collectionscanada.gc.ca/northern-star/*<br>*002036-2100-e.html* |

**Interesting Information:**

*Buxton is in Ontario, Canada. It was founded by Reverend William King, a former slave owner and Presbyterian minister, in 1849 and was the home of runaway and freed slaves. There was a lot of opposition from people living in the region. Buxton consisted of about 9,000 acres. Reverend King built a school and a church in the settlement. He made a lot of rules for the community because he wanted it to be successful and he wanted the people to have pride. Some of the rules were that there could be no alcohol in the settlement, that people had to buy their own homes, and that they had to have a porch, a picket fence, and flowers. Before the Civil War, about 2,000 people lived in Buxton. After the Civil War, many blacks returned to the United States to find loved ones or better jobs or to help in the Reconstruction. Today, about 100 people live in Buxton. In 1999, Buxton was made a National Historic Site. There is a museum there and it has lots of artifacts relating to the Underground Railroad. There is a bell in Buxton that was rung every time a runaway slave reached freedom in Buxton.*

EXAMPLE **4.21**

- **Title:** *Good Masters! Sweet Ladies!*
- **Author:** Laura Amy Schlitz
- **Grade Level:** 5–8
- **Summary:** This series of monologues (and two dialogues) about life in medieval England provides rich information about the children who lived at the time. Interspersed with brief explanations and background information, the monologues prompt many questions that can lead to investigations about medieval life.

If read as a play with selected or assigned parts, students can investigate topics relevant to their character. Otherwise, students can investigate any topic or topics of interest to them.

## Internet Investigation

| |
|---|
| **Character:** *Edgar, the falconer's son* |
| **Topic:** *falconry* |
| **Search Terms:** *falconry, Middle Ages* <br><br> **Internet Sites:** *www.hawk-conservancy.org/histfalc.shtml* <br> *www.pbs.org/falconer/falconry/* <br> *www.americanfalconry.com/beginners.html* <br> *www.n-a-f-a.org/htm/aboutfal_main.htm* |

**Interesting Information:**

- *Falconry has a long history. Birds were used to hunt as far back as 2000 B.C.*
- *In the Middle Ages, falconry was a favorite sport of the kings of England.*
- *Birds of prey were assigned to a rank, and a man could not hunt with a bird that had been assigned to a higher rank than he was.*
- *By the end of the eighteenth century, falconry was not as popular, partly because there were more efficient ways of killing animals for food.*
- *Today, falconry is permitted in most states in the United States but you need a license. Some animal rights activists and environmentalists condemn falconry.*
- *It takes a long time to train a bird.*
- *It takes a lot of money and at least seven years to become a Master Falconer.*

## CONCLUSION

Postreading activities can help students delve more deeply into the literature as they explore ideas, plots, and characters; as they share interpretations with classmates and consider alternative perspectives; and as they plan ways to creatively represent their understandings. The activities also enrich students' interactions with literature by prompting them to make connections across and beyond books as they examine the works of other authors and investigate sources, such as the Internet, for information related to books. The activities help students recognize that rich, deep understanding is often only possible when readers continue to think about books after they have turned the final pages.

### CHAPTER FIVE

# Writing and Bookmaking Activities

## Writing and Bookmaking

### Purposes

- To help students explore and extend their understandings of text
- To help students examine their thinking about what they read
- To prompt creative expression
- To promote an appreciation of authors' ideas and language
- To prompt students to revisit and reconsider literature
- To provide a means for communicating ideas
- To promote an understanding of reading and writing as personally meaningful, communicative acts

### Activities

- Poetic responses
- Literary borrowing
- Multigenre responses
- Pop-up books
- Accordion books
- Fold-up books
- Upside-down books
- Retelling picture books
- Graduated-pages books
- Baggie books
- Paper-bag books

We noted in Chapter One that writing supports students' interactions with literature by allowing them to explore, discover, and develop their thinking. Writing helps students work through and examine their views and uncover new ideas. In describing where her characters come from, children's author Kate DiCamillo (2005) said she looks at and listens to the world around her, but mostly she writes. She writes "to find out" (p. 32). Students, too, can write to find out—find out what they feel, believe, and understand about characters, events, and information in books. Writing can give students time to think deeply and to organize, reorganize, and revise their ideas as they discover what they really think.

Throughout this book, we have described many opportunities for students to write in preparation for or in response to reading literature. Prereading activities, such as anticipation guides and picture carousels, invite students to express their reactions and ideas in writing. Students record predictions based on items contained in book boxes, list and organize ideas generated from reading book bits, and compose quickwrites. They record information in semantic maps, K-W-L charts, and contrast charts. During-reading activities also prompt writing—in literature circles and maps, journals and blogs, character maps and webs, and graphic organizers and charts. Postreading Internet investigations require students to write what they learned about topics of interest to them; multimedia responses include written plans and, oftentimes, written language as one aspect of the presentation; and charts, literary report cards, and other postreading activities prompt students to express their ideas in writing. Many of the writing experiences we have described have been informal, but formal writing experiences are also important for enriching students' interactions with literature.

In this chapter, we share three writing activities that help students explore and extend their understandings of literature, that allow them to examine and creatively express their own thoughts and perspectives, and that promote an appreciation of an author's ideas or language. The activities prompt students to revisit and reconsider the literature as they make decisions about their writing. They support thoughtful and deliberate use of language to construct and express ideas, provide a forum for sharing with peers and others, and move students toward a deeper understanding of reading and writing as exciting, personally meaningful acts. We follow these writing activities with eight ideas for publishing students' writing in individual and class books. Bookmaking is a natural extension of reading the writing of others and a popular means of celebrating students' writing. As background to our activities, we will first briefly describe an approach to teaching writing called the *process approach*, which is widely used in classrooms.

## A Process Approach to Writing

The process approach to writing is based on the work of Janet Emig (1971), Donald Graves (1975), and others who inspired teachers to shift the focus of writing instruction from the end product of writing to the processes of writing. Although processes vary from student to student, task to task, and situation to situation, many classroom teachers are familiar with and teach the following processes: prewriting, drafting, revising, editing, and publishing. Students are sometimes asked to move through their writing as though these processes are sequential steps; however, the processes are not linear. Rather, they are recursive in nature, with writers moving back and forth between them as they write. Writers may revise as they draft, for example, or engage in prewriting after they begin composing. They may edit before or as they revise and draft again after editing. And they may not engage at all in one or more of the processes. As Dyson and Freedman (2003) pointed out, the work on process writing offers a vocabulary for talking about the complex processes involved in writing. Therefore, many teachers find it a useful way to conceptualize and teach writing.

*Prewriting* prepares students for writing. It helps them decide whether they have anything to say, what that might be, how they might say it, and what language (that is, words and phrases) they might use to say it. In addition, it helps students establish purposes for writing and determine the audience for their writing. Many teachers engage students in activities such as brainstorming, outlining, mapping, and discussing to help prepare the students for writing. The activities we share throughout this book can also serve to help students begin to discover and formulate what they have to say.

*Drafting* is the act of writing. Students put their thoughts on paper or key them into a word processor. As they do so, sometimes students realize they do not have enough to say, or that they have too much to say, or that they still are unsure what they want to say. They work to develop their ideas and think about how they want to convey them. In order to support students' focus on ideas and the means by which to express them, teachers generally tell students that they need not concern themselves with spelling, punctuation, and neatness at this early stage of their writing. They also remind students that a first draft is not a final draft—there will be time for revision later—and that the goal now is to get their thoughts down.

*Revising* involves rethinking a work. Gunning (2008) noted that students often think of revising as correcting. In fact, revising "goes to the heart of the piece" (p. 473) and can involve reorganization; adding, eliminating, or changing material; and modifying language to make the work more interesting, colorful, or precise. Often teachers will encourage students to get feedback on their writing, perhaps by conferencing with peers or with the teacher. This feedback informs the revision process.

*Editing* is the process of checking for correctness. Students proofread their work, sometimes with the aid of a form that helps them focus on different elements, such as punctuation, spelling, or sentence structure. Teachers also often suggest that students use peer editors or they structure peer editing opportunities.

**Technology**

*Publishing* is a way of sharing and honoring student work and making it available for real audiences. Student writing can be published in a variety of ways, including posting it on a class web page or on online publishing sites, printing it in school newsletters, reading it aloud in a podcast to be downloaded by peers and others, and constructing individual or class books to be placed in classroom libraries.

The writing activities we share in this chapter include *poetic responses, literary borrowing,* and *multigenre responses.* These are followed by suggestions for constructing *pop-up books, accordion books, fold-up books, upside-down books, retelling picture books, graduated-pages books, baggie books,* and *paper-bag books.*

The purposes of engaging children in these writing and publishing activities are as follows:

- To help students explore and extend their understandings of text
- To help students examine their thinking about what they read
- To prompt creative expression
- To promote an appreciation of authors' ideas and language
- To prompt students to revisit and reconsider literature
- To provide a means for communicating ideas
- To promote an understanding of reading and writing as personally meaningful, communicative acts

# *Poetic Responses*

Writing poetry in response to literature can be a powerful experience that allows students to explore and express their understandings and feelings about a reading selection and that develops a sense of pride in students as they become authors whose words can move others. Teachers can share many forms of poetry, including free verse, haiku, cinquain, diamante, and shape poems. They may have students attend to rhythm, rhyme, and presentation on a page. Here, we share three types of poetic responses—Found poems, I Am poems, and Where I'm From poems—in which students capture in free verse what they feel is the essence of a selection.

*Found poems* are arrangements of language that has been selected from, or "found" in, a reading selection (Dunning & Stafford, 1992). After reading, students reflect on their reaction to or understanding of the selection. They may draw or brainstorm feelings and impressions. They may talk with a peer. They consider what they want to say in response to the selection or how they wish to poetically summarize their understandings. Then, the students return to the text to identify words and phrases that capture their response, looking for language that is appealing, important, or meaningful. Students record words and phrases of their choice and begin to arrange them to form a poem. Recording word and phrase selections on a word processor facilitates the organization and reorganization of the words and phrases. Alternatively, students may write their selections on small strips of paper, which they manipulate as they try different constructions. As students work, they abandon some of their selections and return to the text for new selections. They try several arrangements of the words and phrases and share drafts with a peer or the teacher, revising their poems until they are satisfied. They write their poems in final form, attending to the layout of the words on a page or across pages of a book. They may wish to include illustrations.

**Technology**

Creating a Found poem encourages students to reflect on and examine the language of the author. What phrases in the text evoke strong images or emotions in the reader? What words are unusual, highly relevant, interesting, or telling? What words or phrases summarize the author's intent? How can these words and phrases be used in another way to share reactions to or perceptions of the author's work? What words or phrases capture what the student wants to communicate? Readers select any words and phrases they wish and then organize the language in whatever way suits them. Because students draw entirely from the language of the author, the linguistic demands on the students are lessened. Yet, because students must examine the author's language in order to make choices for use in their own poetry, they engage with rich language. The scaffolding provides support, and the close attention to and use of the author's language provide an opportunity for language development. Thus, Found poems are beneficial for all students, including English learners. Examples 5.1 and 5.2 are poems "found" by students in the language of works of fiction and nonfiction, respectively.

**English learners**

*I Am poems* (adapted from Fisher & Frey, 2003) provide students with a frame for building a poem. Students choose a character in a reading selection and revisit the text to think about the experiences, thoughts, and qualities of the character. Students may be encouraged to brainstorm or create a character web (described in Chapter Three) in preparation for writing their poem. Then, students draft each line in the poem ("I am . . . ," "I feel . . . ," "I wish . . . ," and so on) in the voice of the character. Lines are rearranged in whatever way appeals to the poet. Students share with one another and use their peers' reactions and feedback to revise and edit their poems. The underlined phrases in Example 5.3

are a fourth-grade student's words as she completed each line after reading *The Year of Miss Agnes* by Kirkpatrick Hill. Example 5.4 provides two I Am poems in response to Jack London's *The Call of the Wild*, each written from a different character's perspective.

*Where I'm From poems* also provide a scaffold for students' writing in response to a reading selection. This type of poetic response is based on a poem by George Ella Lyon (Lyon, 1999) in which the refrain "I am from" is repeated as the poet describes elements of her heritage and life, and adapted from Christensen (2000), who had her students write about their lives using the poem as a model. The Where I'm From poem can be used to capture the voice, experiences, and feelings of a character in a story or a contemporary or historical figure in a biography. Example 5.5 shares two students' poems in response to *Out of the Dust* by Karen Hesse.

Each of these three types of poetry provides a scaffold for student writing. When writing a Found poem, students draw entirely on the language of the author, and when writing I Am and Where I'm From poems, students are provided frames on which to build their poems. Thus, all students—including reluctant writers and lower-achieving students—can find writing poetry in response to literature a highly successful experience that enriches their understandings of the reading selections. Likewise, more advanced learners are provided the opportunity to represent perhaps more sophisticated understandings in creative ways through these poems.

## EXAMPLE 5.1

- **Title:** *Virgie Goes to School with Us Boys*
- **Author:** Elizabeth Fitzgerald Howard
- **Grade Level:** K–3
- **Summary:** After President Lincoln's Emancipation Proclamation, former slaves were allowed to attend school. Virgie's brothers walk seven miles to a school opened by the Quakers, and Virgie, a girl, is determined to attend as well. Based on a real family's history, the author is the granddaughter of one of Virgie's brothers.

### Found Poem

*Virgie always asking,*
*"Can I go to school?"*

*Too little.*
*Scarcely big as a field mouse.*
*Girls don't need school.*

*She kept asking and asking.*

*Too little.*
*Scarcely big as a field mouse.*
*Girls don't need school.*

*Virgie always asking.*

*All free people*
  *need learning.*
*You can go to school with the boys.*
*Free.*

EXAMPLE **5.2**

- **Title:** *I Face the Wind*
- **Author:** Vicki Cobb
- **Grade Level:** 1–3
- **Summary:** In this Robert F. Siebert Honor Book, the author provides information about the wind and suggests activities that help children understand scientific concepts.

### Found Poem

| Student 1: | Student 2: |
|---|---|
| *Strong wind* | *Your hair blows.* |
| *You can't see* | *You lose your hat!* |
| *You can feel* | *Why?* |
| *This force that's pushing you.* | *Air is real stuff.* |
| *Air is real stuff.* | *Air is heavier than nothing.* |
| *Molecules—gazillions of moving* | *Experiment. Imagine.* |
| *air molecules.* | *Can you feel it?* |
| *The push of the wind.* | *Yay!* |

EXAMPLE **5.3**

- **Title:** *The Year of Miss Agnes*
- **Author:** Kirkpatrick Hill
- **Grade Level:** 2–5
- **Summary:** Frederika and her classmates in a one-room schoolhouse in remote Alaska find that their new teacher is very different from the others who have come and gone so quickly. She wears pants, shares music, reads stories aloud, and finds the strengths in each of her students. She also insists that Frederika's deaf sister attend school. Readers get a glimpse of Alaska's geography, history, and culture.

### I Am Poem

I am _Frederika_.
I want _to go to school_.
I wonder _who our new teacher will be_.
I hear _music from her record player_.
I see _a woman in pants_!
I am _Frederika_.
I pretend _I am from another time_.
I feel _I am inside the book she reads_.
I touch _the big map on the wall_.
I worry _our teacher will hate the smell of fish_.
I cry _when I think about her leaving us_.
I am _Frederika_.
I understand _why I must learn arithmetic_.
I say _my sister is deaf_.
I dream _that I will see the world_.
I try _not to cry_.
I hope _our teacher will stay_.
I am _Fred_.

EXAMPLE 5.4

- **Title:** *The Call of the Wild*
- **Author:** Jack London
- **Grade Level:** 5–8
- **Summary:** Buck is a well-cared-for family dog who is removed from his comfortable home in California to serve as a sled dog in the Alaskan wilderness. John Thornton, a prospector, becomes his master.

### *I Am Poem*

I am *John Thornton*.
I wonder *why Buck goes away for a long time*.
I hear *wolves howling*.
I see *a valley filled with gold*.
I want *to become rich*.
I am *John Thornton*.
I pretend *to fight my dog*.
I feel *calloused hands*.
I touch *yellow gold*.
I worry *that my dog will get hurt*.
I cry *when my leg gets hurt from the snow*.
I am *John Thornton*.
I understand *my dog*.
I say *"You devil."*
I dream *of being rich*.
I try *to become rich*.
I hope *to be successful*.
I am *John Thornton*.

I am *Buck*.
I wonder *why the snow falls*.
I hear *wolves howling*.
I see *snow*.
I want *a loving master*.
I am *Buck*.
I pretend *to be a wolf sometimes*.
I feel *the cold snow*.
I touch *the hard ground*.
I worry *about my master leaving me*.
I cry *to the heavens*.
I am *Buck*.
I understand *the call of the wild*.
I say *"Bark!"*
I dream *about cavemen*.
I try *to help my master*.
I hope *to catch a moose and eat it*.
I am *Buck*.

EXAMPLE 5.5

- **Title:** *Out of the Dust*
- **Author:** Karen Hesse
- **Grade Level:** 4–6

■ **Summary:** Thirteen-year-old Billie Jo experiences the Depression and the dust storms that ravage Oklahoma and the Dust Bowl during the 1930s. In a tragic accident, her mother and infant brother die and Billie Jo and her father ultimately find their way toward one another.

### *Where I'm From Poem*

**Student 1:**

*I am from wheat fields, from farmland*
  *From a little house, a tractor, and apple trees.*

*I am from a redheaded daddy, a man of the sod, who always wanted a boy.*
*And a Ma, a Ma who lies on the hill.*

*I am from the piano, from moving my fingers across the keys*
  *From rhythm, from music, from a Ma who played and*
  *Taught me to play.*

*I am from dust so thick we cannot see, we cannot breathe,*
  *Tearing up the fields*
*From waves and waves*
*And waves of dust*
*From days and days of dust.*
*And drought.*
*Again.*

*I am from horror, from grief so deep I feel everything and nothing,*
  *from emptiness, from terrible pain.*
*I am from kerosene by the stove, from fire.*
*I am from a dead mother and a dead brother.*
*I am from a silent, distant father.*

*I am from scarred hands, a scarred land, a scarred life, scarred love.*

*I am from guilt. I am from anger.*
*I am from running away and finding nowhere to go.*

*I am from forgiveness and from hope.*

*I am from this land.*

**Student 2:**

*I am from dust and dust*

*And dust*
*I am from wind and drought*
*I am from death.*

*I am from accidents and fire that destroys so much outside of me and*
*Inside of me.*
*I am from loneliness and pain.*

*I am from the farmlands of Oklahoma.*
*This is where I belong.*

# *Literary Borrowing*

Literature serves as a powerful model for writing. Readers acquire ideas for characters, plots, text structures, and language from the writing of others. Lancia (1997) discovered that spontaneous "literary borrowing" is common among young students as they become writers and has maintained that such borrowing should be recognized and valued for its role in writing development. It also can be used to support students' interactions with literature.

Students may borrow different aspects of the books they hear or read. They may borrow an entire story or the information they learned from a work of non-fiction, retelling or summarizing the literature in their own words. In doing so, students identify important events or ideas for inclusion in their writing and they make decisions about organization of information. Reconstruction of a text has been found to increase students' comprehension (Brown, 1975; Duke & Pearson, 2002) and enhance students' concepts of story structure and their language (Koskinen, Gambrell, Kapinus, & Heathington, 1988; Morrow, 1985).

In literary borrowing, students may write a new adventure for a familiar character. They think carefully about the character, considering the character's habits, language, personality, experiences, and relationships. They develop richer understandings of the character as they place him or her in a novel situation. Activities in this book that focus on understanding characters serve as excellent prewriting experiences for students who wish to write new episodes for known characters.

Students may also borrow a plot, but change the details. For example, students may use the plot of *The Little Red Hen* by Vera Southgate to write their own story in which a hen is preparing a salad rather than baking bread. As in the original, they include the steps for preparing the meal, the request for help, and the refusal of other animals to assist. Similarly, students may borrow the plot, but change the perspective from which the story is told. In the case of *The Little Red Hen*, students may retell the story from the point of view of the chicks.

The patterns in books such as *Over in the Meadow*, retold by John Langstaff, may be borrowed to write companion pieces, such as *Over in the Forest* and *Over in the Desert*. Students may study the cumulative patterns in books such as *The House that Jack Built* by David Cutts, *I Know an Old Lady* by Rose Bonne, and *Here Is the African Savanna* and *Here Is the Arctic Winter*, both by Madeleine Dunphy, to write their own cumulative pattern books.

Alphabet books and counting books also provide patterns students may emulate. Books that repeat a linguistic structure, such as Kate Petty's *I Didn't Know that Crocodiles Yawn to Keep Cool* in which the phrase "I didn't know that . . . " is used repeatedly, also provide a pattern for students to use. Example 5.6 shares one student's use of this pattern to share his response to *Living Color* by Steve Jenkins.

## EXAMPLE 5.6

- **Title:** *Living Color*
- **Author:** Steve Jenkins
- **Grade Level:** 3–5
- **Summary:** The author artist shares some of the world's brightly colored creatures and explains how their colors contribute to their survival.

### *I Didn't Know That . . .*

*I didn't know that color in animals has meaning!*
*I didn't know that the white uakaris monkey with the brightest red face is the one in charge.*

*I didn't know that poisonous caterpillars are often brightly colored.*
*I didn't know that the giant green anemone is a colorless animal and that algae*
    *make its body look green.*
*I didn't know that some animals change color to show their emotions.*
*I didn't know that some animals use their color to warn other animals away from*
    *their territory.*
*I didn't know that some animals' color is a clue about their diet.*
*I didn't know that an animal's color can attract a mate.*
*I didn't know that animals are so interesting!*

## Multigenre Responses

A multigenre response, as the name suggests, is a collection of different genres of writing composed in response to a work of literature. When students develop a multigenre response, they consider not only what they wish to say but also how they wish to say it. Key is that, although several different genres are used, they together form a coherent piece. As Romano (2000, pp. x–xi) noted, "A multigenre paper is composed of many genres and subgenres, each piece self-contained, making a point of its own, yet connected by theme or topic and sometimes by language, images and content."

An excellent example of multigenre literature is *The Man Who Went to the Far Side of the Moon: The Story of Apollo 11 Astronaut Michael Collins* by Bea Uusma Schyffert. The text contains journal entries, drawings, photographs, lists, diagrams, and exposition. Readers get a rich, multilayered view of the experiences of Astronaut Collins who remained aboard the spacecraft while his colleagues took humankind's first steps on the moon. *The Invention of Hugo Cabret* by Brian Selznick, who won the Caldecott Medal for this work, is another extraordinary example of multigenre literature. Much of the story is told through pictures, some that work like a flip book, and much is told through prose. Lynne Rae Perkins won the Newbery Medal for her multigenre work *Criss Cross,* which combines narrative, haiku and other poetry, drawings, photographs, and a question-and-answer format to tell a moving, humorous coming-of-age story.

To develop a multigenre response to a work of literature, students engage in prewriting activities such as brainstorming, sketching, listing, and making semantic maps to discover what they wish to say and to begin organizing their thoughts. They consider a variety of genres, and select several that they believe hold promise. Possible genres include narratives, poetry, cartoons, obituaries, news releases, letters, skits, interviews, photo collages, travel posters or brochures, graphs, job applications, and resumés. Working individually or in pairs, students draft their responses. The teacher ensures time for sharing so that students can benefit from hearing the ideas of peers as well as obtaining feedback on their work at several points in their composing. Students should have opportunities for feedback on self-contained sections of their work as well as on the collection as a whole, including its organization. They revise their ideas and their choice of genres, and ultimately they make decisions about how to formally present their work. They might produce an electronic presentation, mural, book, or poster. Or students might record each individual genre response on a separate piece of paper and insert them all into a box, which becomes a "memory box" for the book.

Technology

Students may work in different grouping configurations to develop a multi-genre response. As we noted previously, each student may write his or her own multigenre response or work with a partner. Example 5.7 shares a collaborative multigenre response written by two sixth-graders. They used poetry, a want ad, exposition, and a letter to express their response to *Being Caribou: Five Months on Foot with an Arctic Herd* by Karsten Heuer. Alternatively, the teacher may have each student respond to a work of literature using a different genre, and then have small groups combine their individual pieces into a multigenre work. Based on students' strengths or needs, teachers may assign the genres to students, or they may provide students with several options and allow students to select those of greatest interest to them. Students work with peers to merge their individual contributions into a cohesive whole. Example 5.8 shares the prompts a third-grade teacher used with a group of students. In this case, each student randomly drew a prompt from a box and then developed a response. Eventually, all the responses were posted on a bulletin board dedicated to the literature. Students worked together to organize the display.

## EXAMPLE 5.7

- **Title:** *Being Caribou: Five Months on Foot with an Arctic Herd*
- **Author:** Karsten Heuer
- **Grade Level:** 3–6
- **Summary:** This book chronicles the five-month trek of a scientist/park ranger and his wife as they follow a herd of caribou to their calving grounds in Alaska's Arctic National Wildlife Refuge. The text of the couple's rigorous journey is accompanied by photographs they took along the way.

### Multigenre Response

*Caribou*
*Where are you?*
*I worry*
*You'll become too few.*

*Wanted!*
*Intelligent human beings*
*Who understand*
*The value of wildlife*

*Caribou have, for 27,000 years, been migrating along the same trails in the Arctic Circle to their calving grounds. Sometimes covering 90 miles in a single day, they head north away from wolves, grizzlies, and insects to bear their young. Calves can stand within five minutes after their birth and spend days playing with their mothers. The play leads to bonding, which is crucial for their survival. The calving grounds have been targeted by oil companies for drilling.*

*Dear Senator:*
*Who will protect us?*
*Who will protect our young?*
*How will we survive?*
*Please use your voice and your vote to save us.*
*Sincerely,*
*The Caribou*

EXAMPLE 5.8

- **Title:** *Flossie & the Fox*
- **Author:** Patricia C. McKissack
- **Grade Level:** K–3
- **Summary:** Warning young Flossie to keep watch for an egg-stealing fox, Big Mama sends her off with a basket of eggs to give to a neighbor. Flossie walks through the woods where she is soon confronted by the fox. Clever Flossie frustrates his every attempt to convince her who he is.

Write a detailed description of the appearance of the fox.

Write a want ad in which Flossie seeks to purchase a larger basket to carry eggs.

Write directions from Flossie's home to the McCutchin Place.

Write an informational poster alerting farmers to beware of foxes.

Write a diary entry by the fox after his encounter with Flossie.

Write a recipe for cooking eggs.

Write a letter of thanks from Miz Viola to Flossie and her grandmother.

## Pop-Up Books

Although student writing may be published in a number of forms, we offer in the remainder of this chapter a variety of ways that students can construct books for sharing their writing. Books may be coauthored, as when many students each contribute a page, or they may be individual works. Ideally, student books are placed in a classroom library or other location where they are visible and accessible. They are intended to be read!

Pop-up books are eye catching and easy to construct. Students enjoy the three-dimensional nature of these books. To make a pop-up book, follow these simple directions:

**1.** Fold a piece of paper in half. Construction paper provides the best thickness and support for the pop-up pictures, but copy paper will do. Make two cuts of equal length about one inch apart into the creased edge of the paper.

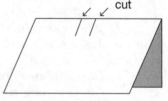

**2.** Open the paper so the two halves form a right angle. Pull the cut section through and fold it inward.

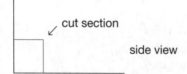

**3.** Paste a picture onto the cut section as shown. You will probably want to have your students draw background pictures prior to pasting the pop-ups onto the page. The text also should be written on the paper prior to pasting and is typically on the bottom half of the paper.

Several pop-up figures may be placed on one page. Their sizes and placements can vary by making shorter or longer cuts and by making the cuts closer together or farther apart. Each page should be constructed separately.

**4.** After each page is constructed, stack the folded pages in order, and glue them together.

*The Three Bears*

# Accordion Books

Accordion books provide an excellent opportunity for collaborative writing and group problem solving. Summarizing a story or utilizing a question-and-answer format or an "I didn't know that . . . " or other pattern, each student composes a page of the book on tagboard. The boards are lined up end to end and taped or tied together in sequence. Books may stand freely on counters accordion-style or be folded for placement on a library shelf.

To ensure a cohesive product, group members should thoroughly discuss and agree on the text and illustrations prior to making individual assignments. If students do not discuss details, they run the risk of having a final product that lacks continuity and is clumsy. For example, one page may be written in the present tense and the next in the past tense, or a character may be blond on one page and brunette on the next.

## Fold-Up Books

Students can create a book that opens like a conventional book by folding and cutting a single sheet of paper. The size of the book will depend on the size of the paper used. Some students will enjoy making big books using butcher paper, and others will prefer to make miniatures using an 8½ × 11 piece of paper. Directions must be followed carefully.

**1.** Fold a rectangular piece of paper into eighths as shown, pressing firmly on the creases. Open the paper, then refold the opposite direction on the same folds, again creasing firmly.

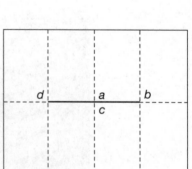

**2.** Fold the paper in half and cut on the center line as shown.

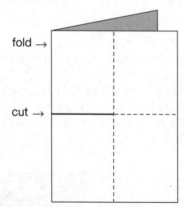

**3.** Open the paper. Lift points *a* and *c*, pulling them upward and away from each other so that points *b* and *d* come together. This will be difficult if folds are not well creased.

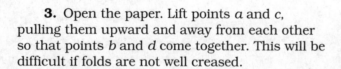

Your paper should look like this from the top:

**4.** Bring all flaps together to form the book. Crease all folds.

**5.** Students write and illustrate the pages of their book.

Fold-up books can be unfolded and photocopied to make a class set. Additionally, they can be unfolded, turned text side down, and refolded so a second book can be created on the same piece of paper.

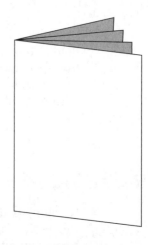

## Upside-Down Books

This type of book is useful when contrasting ideas are discussed or suggested by a piece of literature. One idea is written on one side of a piece of paper, and the contrasting idea is written upside down on the reverse side. For example, students may write contrasting information about Earth's poles after reading *North Pole South Pole* by Nancy Smiler Levinson. In the steps below, students write about both a terrible day and a wonderful day after reading *Alexander and the Terrible, Horrible, No Good, Very Bad Day* by Judith Viorst.

**1.** Each student completes the prompt "It was a terrible, horrible, no good, very bad day when . . ." on a piece of paper and illustrates it.

It was a terrible...

**2.** Upside down and on the reverse side of the paper, each student completes and illustrates the second prompt, "It was a wonderful, delightful, marvelous, fantastic day when. . . ." If the teacher or students prefer, students may complete the second picture and narration on a separate piece of paper and the two pages may be pasted onto a sheet of construction paper, one on the front and the other upside down on the back.

It was a wonderful...

**3.** All student papers are collected and stacked together, the same side up. In other words, all the "terrible day" sentences and illustrations are facing up, and all the "wonderful day" sentences and illustrations are facing down (and are upside down). An appropriate title page should be added to the front and the back. Bind the pages with staples, ribbons, brads, or whatever is available. When the book is read in one direction, it describes very bad days. When the book is turned over and upside down, it describes wonderful days.

Our Terrible Days

Our Wonderful Days

Information recorded in a contrast chart can provide ideas for an upside-down book. For example, the advantages and disadvantages of being two inches tall were listed in a contrast chart for *Stuart Little* by E. B. White in Chapter Two of this book. Students may create an upside-down book based on this chart with one side of the paper illustrating "A good thing about being two inches tall is . . ." and the reverse side of the paper illustrating "A bad thing about being two inches tall is . . . ."

## *Retelling Picture Books*

Retelling picture books allow students to retell stories with the help of attached characters that can be moved on and off the pages of the book. First, settings are identified and illustrations are drawn, painted, or cut and pasted onto pieces of paper that become the pages of the book. A title page is created that includes a pocket in which characters may be stored. The pages are then bound together by any means.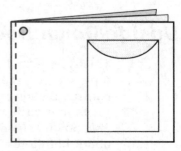

Next, characters are drawn onto tagboard and cut out. A hole is punched in each character, and a ribbon is tied through the hole. The other end of the ribbon is tied through a hole punched in the upper left-hand corner of the book. The ribbons must be long enough so that the students can move the characters freely. Three feet is a good length.

Students may then move the characters onto each page of the book as they retell the story.

One student teacher constructed a retelling picture book with a class of kindergarteners. She had each of her students make the following illustrations for *Goldilocks and the Three Bears* by Lorinda Bryan Cauley, on 12 × 18-inch pieces of construction paper:

Page 1:  the bears' house in the middle of a forest
Page 2:  three bowls of porridge with the words *Papa, Mama,* and *Baby* written on them
Page 3:  three chairs and a stairway
Page 4:  three beds

After a title page was created and the pages were bound together, each student drew a picture of Goldilocks on tagboard and cut it out. Each also drew the three bears, cut them out, and pasted them together side by side so they could be moved about as a single entity. Goldilocks and the bears were then connected by ribbons to a corner of the book as just described.

When the children retold the story, they removed the characters from the pocket on the title page, opened the first page of the book, and moved the appropriate characters onto the page. On page 1, the bears were moved from the house into the forest to go for a walk. Goldilocks was moved onto the page to discover the bears' open house. On page 2, Goldilocks was moved from bowl to bowl before finding Baby Bear's porridge just right to eat. The students continued retelling the story while moving the characters from page to page.

A retelling picture book provides students with a structure for retelling a story, and the scenes serve as reminders for each part of the story. Retelling picture books are very motivational and promote language development. They are adaptable to many grade levels. Older students may make books for younger ones or may develop a retelling picture book for a section of a novel they are reading.

# *Graduated-Pages Books*

Graduated-pages books are especially useful for making reference-type books because the pages are laid out so the reader can flip quickly to a topic of interest. The steps for making a graduated-pages book are as follows.

**1.** Decide on the number of pages in the book, including the title page. Divide the number of pages by two to determine the number of sheets of paper needed. For example, if you plan on an eight-page book, you will need four sheets of paper.

**2.** Set the papers in an overlapping stack, leaving one-half to one inch of each paper exposed (as shown on the right).

**3.** Fold the stack of papers as shown. Staple at the folded edge, if desired (as shown below).

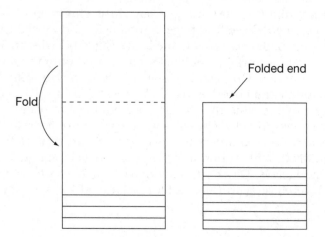

**4.** Students label each page at the exposed edge. This label provides the topic addressed on the page and allows readers to quickly find information.

After reading or listening to a book or several books about bats, for example, students might write what they have learned in a graduated-pages book, labeling each page with a main idea and sharing drawings and details that can be viewed or read when the book is opened to the appropriate page. For example, one page might be labeled "Bats are mammals." Drawings and a discussion of the classification or physical characteristics of bats would be found on this page. Another page might be labeled "Bats use echolocation." A description of bats' use of echoes to locate food would be found on this page.

Books can be constructed either to open upwards, as shown in the diagrams above, or to open to the left like a more conventional book as shown here.

All
about
Bats!

*By Billy T.*

# Baggie Books

Baggie books are made with resealable plastic bags, cardstock, and tape. Pages of the book are created on cardstock and then inserted into baggies that are taped together at the bottom end. These books have several advantages. First, they are reusable because the cardstock pages can be removed from the baggies and replaced with new pages. Second, objects related to the writing can be slipped into the baggies. For example, if students write a book in response to *Flowers Fruits Seeds* by Jerome Wexler, they can put various seeds in their baggies. Third, the baggie serves as a laminate to the cardstock pages, and students can write on the baggie with erasable markers, allowing opportunities for interaction with the content of the text.

Sandwich-size baggies are commonly used in making baggie books, but larger baggies work well too. After determining the baggie size, the teacher cuts cardstock so it fits comfortably into the baggie. Cardstock is preferable to paper because its stiffness makes it easier to slide into and out of the baggie. The steps for constructing baggie books are as follows:

**1.** Students write and illustrate the pages of their book, using the front and back sides of the cardstock.

**2.** Students tape baggies together. Each baggie will hold one piece of cardstock, or two pages of the book. Thus, four baggies will yield an eight-page book. Wide tape is most effective for taping the baggies together, and teachers often make colored tape available to their students. Some teachers suggest that the students staple the baggies before binding the pages of their book with tape. If the pages are stapled, holes result, which is a problem only if the students want to put a very fine material, such as sand, into their baggies. If the pages are only taped, the teacher will need to support young children to ensure that all the baggies make contact with the tape. To do this, the baggies should be laid on top of each other in a slightly staggered fashion as shown. Alternatively, baggies can be taped together two at a time. Then each pair is taped to another pair, and each set is taped to another set until all the baggies are taped together. This technique, however, requires more tape than the teacher may wish to use.

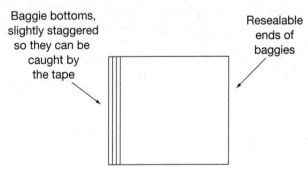

Baggie bottoms, slightly staggered so they can be caught by the tape

Resealable ends of baggies

**3.** Cardstock pages are inserted into the baggies, along with any objects the students choose to include.

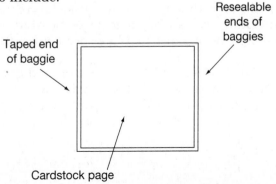

Resealable ends of baggies

Taped end of baggie

Cardstock page

## *Paper-Bag Books*

Paper-bag books are constructed with lunch-size paper bags of any color that are stacked and folded in half. This will result in pages that have an opening at the edge (the mouths of the bags) and pages that have a flap (the bottoms of the bags), both of which make fun hiding places for additional information. Here are the steps for constructing a paper-bag book.

**1.** Stack several flat unopened bags, with the folded bottom facing up. Alternate the direction of the opening of the bags from right to left, as in the illustration below. The number of bags used depends on the number of pages desired.

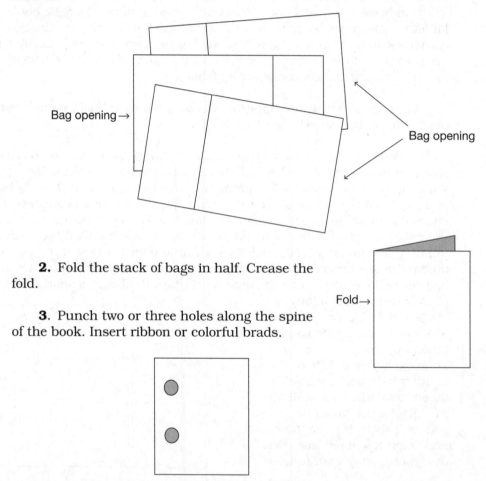

Bag opening →

Bag opening

**2.** Fold the stack of bags in half. Crease the fold.

Fold→

**3.** Punch two or three holes along the spine of the book. Insert ribbon or colorful brads.

**4.** Add text and illustrations, using markers or construction paper, to each page. Use the flaps that are on some pages to create a "lift the flap" effect. Use the open mouths that are on some pages to insert additional text or illustrations on separate pieces of paper that have been cut to fit inside the opening.

Paper-bag books are ideal for question-and-answer structures. Questions are written on the pages of the book and answers are provided under a flap or on separate pieces of paper that are in the mouth of a bag.

## CONCLUSION

Beach, Appleman, Hynds, and Wilhem (2006) lamented that much of the writing about literature that occurs in classrooms is in the form of responses to worksheets, book report summaries, and five-paragraph essays. The problems with these forms of written response is that often they focus on right answers, and they fail to foster exploratory thinking about a book, inspire students to have a genuine purpose for their writing, or provide students with an audience other than the teacher. The activities we shared in this chapter were intended to support students' thoughtful responses to literature as they work to formulate their ideas and write for genuine purposes and for real audiences.

# Afterword

We hope that teachers will find the activities described in this book useful for promoting meaningful interactions with literature and inspiring a love of reading in their students. Before teachers incorporate these activities into their literature programs, however, we would like to issue a few cautions.

First, it is important that teachers know their students and make instructional decisions based on students' interests and needs. As teachers who differentiate instruction know, activities that are appropriate for some groups of

students may be less valuable for others. For example, some students may have considerable background knowledge on a particular topic and so will need less time devoted to building background knowledge prior to interacting with the selection. Other students may have little background knowledge on the topic and will profit from participation in a number of prereading activities. Likewise, reluctant readers will benefit from activities that spark their interest and establish connections between their lives and the literature.

Second, teachers should not be surprised if students do not engage in a grand conversation the first time an activity is attempted. Many students have experienced only gentle (or not so gentle!) inquisitions in school settings. They have learned that there is only one correct answer, that the most verbal students will provide it, or that if they wait long enough the teacher will provide it. This is especially true of older students who have had more time to learn these lessons. Given these expectations, it is not likely that all students will respond enthusiastically to the activities at first. Teachers may need to attempt the activities several times before achieving participation from everyone, while at the same time building trust and new expectations in their students.

Third, these activities should not be used as worksheets that are to be completed independently and collected for a grade. They are intended to arouse curiosity, spark conversation, activate background knowledge, focus attention on themes or language, promote comprehension, encourage reflection on issues or events encountered in books, and help students find literature selections personally meaningful. Few independently completed worksheets achieve these goals. They can be achieved, however, through meaningful interaction among students and with the teacher.

Fourth, literature activities should not be overused. We know one teacher who implemented several prereading activities before every chapter of a novel. We were not surprised when she told us that her students disliked the novel and lost enthusiasm for the activities. Anything can be overdone. Teachers should exercise reason when using literature activities before, during, and after reading. Sometimes it is most appropriate to use none at all.

Finally, teachers should provide students with many opportunities to read, listen to, and talk about literature in the classroom throughout the day and in many contexts. These opportunities, along with an extensive classroom library, will go a long way toward promoting a love of reading.

# Internet Resources

## SELECTED AUTHOR WEBSITES

**http://lsparkreader.livejournal.com/** (Linda Sue Park)

**www.almaada.com** (Alma Flor Ada)

**www.avi-writer.com** (Avi)

**www.ayles.com** (Jim Aylesworth)

**www.bernardmost.com** (Bernard Most)

**www.betsybyars.com** (Betsy Byars)

**www.eric-carle.com** (Eric Carle)

**www.ezra-jack-keats.org** (Ezra Jack Keats)

**www.jacquelinewoodson.com/** (Jacqueline Woodson)

**www.janbrett.com** (Jan Brett)

**www.jeancraigheadgeorge.com** (Jean Craighead George)

**www.judyblume.com** (Judy Blume)

**www.loislowry.com** (Lois Lowry)

**www.pammunozryan.com/books.html** (Pamela Muñoz Ryan)

**www.patriciapolacco.com** (Patricia Polacco)

**www.seymoursimon.com/** (Seymour Simon)

**www.sharoncreech.com** (Sharon Creech)

**www.terabithia.com** (Katherine Paterson)

**www.theinventionofhugocabret.com** (Brian O. Selznick)

**www.willhobbsauthor.com** (Will Hobbs)

## WEBSITES WITH LISTS OF AWARD-WINNING CHILDREN'S LITERATURE

**www.ailanet.org**
> Provides a list of the winners of the American Indian Youth Literature Awards presented by the American Indian Library Association to honor outstanding writing and illustrations by and about American Indians

**www.ala.org/ala/alsc/awardsscholarships/childrensnotable/notablebooklist/currentnotable.htm**
> Provides a list of books selected by the Association for Library Service to Children as the best in children's literature

**www.ala.org/alsc/belpre.html**
Provides information about the Pura Belpré Award for Latino/a authors and illustrators for books best portraying the Latino/a cultural experience and a list of award winners

**www.ala.org/alsc/caldecott.html**
Provides information about the Caldecott Medal for the illustrator of the most distinguished picture book and a list of award winners

**www.ala.org/alsc/newbery.html**
Provides information about the Newbery Medal for distinguished children's literature and a list of award winners

**www.ala.org/ala/pr2004/prfeb2004/SchneiderFamilyBookAw.htm**
Provides information about the Schneider Family book award for books depicting the disability experience and list of award winners

**www.ala.org/srrt/csking/**
Provides information about the Coretta Scott King Award for illustrators and authors of African descent whose books promote an understanding and appreciation of the American Dream and a list of award winners

**www.apalaweb.org/awards/awards.htm**
Provides a list of the winners of the Asian/Pacific American Awards for Literature given by the Asian/Pacific American Librarians Association; the prizes promote Asian/Pacific American culture and heritage and are awarded based on literary and artistic merit

**www.cde.ca.gov/ci/sc/ll/**
Provides a list of outstanding science- and mathematics-related literature for children and adolescents

**www.dawcl.com**
Provides a database of award-winning children's literature

**www.hbook.com/bghb/**
Lists the winners of the Boston Globe-Horn Book Award for children's and young adult literature. The winning titles must be published in the United States but they may be written or illustrated by citizens of any country

**www.meoc.us**
Provides a list of Middle East Award winners—books for children and adults that contribute to an understanding of the Middle East

**www.nationalbook.org/index.html**
Provides lists of winners of the National Book Award

**www.ncte.org/about/awards/sect/elem/106877.htm**
Provides information about the Orbis Pictus Nonfiction Award and a list of award winners

**www.nsta.org/pubs/sc/ostblist.asp**
Provides a list of Outstanding Science Trade Books for Children

**www.reading.org/associations/awards/childrens_ira.html**
Provides a list of Children's and Young Adults' Book Awards given by the International Reading Association for an author's first or second published work written for children or young adults

**www.reading.org/resources/tools/choices_childrens.html**
Provides a list of books selected by children as favorites

**www.reading.org/resources/tools/choices_teachers.html**
Provides a list of books for children selected by teachers, reading specialists, and librarians

**www.reading.org/resources/tools/choices_young_adults.html**
Provides a list of books selected by adolescents as favorites

**www.socialstudies.org/awards/woodson/**
Provides a list of distinguished social science books that treat topics related to ethnic minorities and race relations sensitively and accurately

**www.socialstudies.org/resources/notable/**
Provides a list of notable trade books in the social studies

## OTHER WEBSITES OF INTEREST

**http://rite.ed.qut.edu.au/oz-teachernet/projects/book-rap/iondex1.html**
Provides opportunities for online literature discussions with students around the globe

**www.storylineonline.net**
Provides streaming video of actors reading aloud children's books

**http://wikiblogedu.org/**
Provides information and videos on ways to integrate wikis and blogs into the classroom

**http://wik.ed.uiuc.edu/index.php/Wiki_in_a_K-12_classroom**
Shares examples of uses of wikis in the classroom

**www.bibliofind.com**
Locates out-of-print, hard-to-find, and rare books

**www.bookfinder.com**
Locates new and used books

**www.acs.ucalgary.ca/~dkbrown/index.html**
Provides information about Internet resources related to books for children and adults

**www.cbcbooks.org**
Provides information about the Children's Book Council which, among other activities, sponsors Young People's Poetry Week and Children's Book Week

**www.ed.gov/teachers/how/tech/international/index.html**
Provides information and ideas for teachers who want to have their students engage in Internet projects with students around the world

**www.googlelittrips.org/**
Shares Google Maps projects that provide maps of a character's travels as well as additional information, photos, and links related to a work of literature

**www.hbook.com**
Provides information about books for children and young adults

**www.icdlbooks.org**
Provides a wealth of resources for educators, librarians, and families, including books from around the world and in a variety of languages that can be read online

**www.poets.org**
The website of the Academy of American Poets whose mission it is to foster the appreciation of contemporary poetry

**www.readwritethink.org/**
Provides lesson plans and related materials for language arts teachers

# References

Ada, A. F. (1993). *My name is Maria Isabel.* New York: Atheneum.

Al-Hazza, T. C., & Bucher, K. T. (2008). Building Arab Americans' cultural identity and acceptance with children's literature. *The Reading Teacher, 62,* 210–219.

Allington, R. (1980). Teacher interruption behaviors during primary-grade oral reading. *Journal of Educational Psychology, 72,* 371–377.

Allington, R. (1984). Content coverage and contextual reading in reading groups. *Journal of Reading Behavior, 16,* 85–96.

Allington, R. (1994). The schools we have. The schools we need. *The Reading Teacher, 48,* 14–29.

Almasi, J. (1995). The nature of fourth graders' sociocognitive conflicts in peer-led and teacher-led discussions of literature. *Reading Research Quarterly, 30,* 314–351.

Almasi, J. (1996). A new view of discussion. In L. Gambrell & J. Almasi (Eds.), *Lively discussions! Fostering engaged reading* (pp. 2–24). Newark, DE: International Reading Association.

Almasi, J. F., O'Flahavan, J. F., & Arya, P. (2001). A comparative analysis of student and teacher development in more and less proficient discussions of literature. *Reading Research Quarterly, 36,* 96–120.

Anderson, L. W. (Ed.), Krathwohl, D. R. (Ed.), Airasian, P. W., Cruikshank, K. A., Mayer, R. E., Pintrich, P. R., Raths, J., & Wittrock, M. C. (2001). *A taxonomy for learning, teaching, and assessing: A revision of Bloom's Taxonomy of Educational Objectives* (complete edition). New York: Longman.

Anderson, R. (1984). Role of the reader's schema in comprehension, learning, and memory. In R. Anderson, J. Osborn, & R. Tierney (Eds.), *Learning to read in American schools: Basal readers and content texts.* Hillsdale, NJ: Erlbaum.

Anderson, R., Hiebert, E., Scott, J., & Wilkinson, I. (1985). *Becoming a nation of readers: The report of the Commission on Reading.* Washington, DC: The National Institute of Education, U.S. Department of Education.

Athanases, S. Z. (1998). Diverse learners, diverse texts: Exploring identity and difference through literary encounters. *Journal of Literacy Research, 30,* 273–296.

Atwater, R., & Atwater, F. (1966). *Mr. Popper's penguins.* New York: Little, Brown.

Au, K. H. (2002). Multicultural factors and the effective instruction of students of diverse backgrounds. In A. E. Farstrup & S. J. Samuels (Eds.), *What research has to say about reading instruction* (3rd ed., pp. 392–413). Newark, DE: International Reading Association.

Au, K. H. (2003). Balanced literacy instruction: Implications for students of diverse backgrounds. In J. Flood, D. Lapp, J. R. Squire, & J. M. Jensen (Eds.), *Handbook of research on teaching the English language arts* (2nd ed., pp. 955–966). Mahwah, NJ: Erlbaum.

August, D., & Shanahan, T. (Eds.). (2006). *Developing literacy in second-language learners: Report of the National Literacy Panel on language-minority children and youth.* Mahwah, NJ: Erlbaum.

Avi. (2002). *Crispin: The cross of lead.* New York: Hyperion.

Avi. (2007). *Iron thunder.* New York: Hyperion.

Babbitt, N. (1975). *Tuck everlasting.* New York: Farrar, Straus & Giroux.

Barone, D. (1989). Young children's written responses to literature: The relationship between written response and orthographic knowledge. In S. McCormick & J. Zutell (Eds.), *Cognitive and social perspectives for literacy research and instruction* (pp. 371–379). Chicago: National Reading Conference.

Barone, D. (1990). The written responses of young children: Beyond comprehension to story understanding. *The New Advocate, 3* (1), 49–56.

Baumann, J. F., & Bergeron, B. S. (1993). Story map instruction using children's literature: Effects on first graders' comprehension of central narrative elements. *Journal of Reading Behavior, 25,* 407–437.

Beach, R. (1993). *Reader-response theories.* Urbana, IL: National Council of Teachers of English.

Beach, R., Appleman, D., Hynds, S., & Wilhelm, J. (2006). *Teaching literature to adolescents.* Mahwah, NJ: Erlbaum.

Bean, T. W. (2000). Reading in the content areas: Social constructivist dimensions. In M. L. Kamil, P. B. Mosenthal, P. D. Pearson, & R. Barr (Eds.), *Handbook of reading research, volume II* (pp. 629–644). Mahwah, NJ: Erlbaum.

Beeler, S. B. (1998). *Throw your tooth on the roof.* Boston: Houghton Mifflin.

Berger, M. (2003). *Spinning spiders.* New York: HarperCollins.

Bird, L. (1988). Reading comprehension redefined through literature study: Creating worlds from the printed page. *The California Reader, 21,* 9–14.

Bloom, B. (1956). *Taxonomy of educational objectives: Handbook I, cognitive domain.* New York: D. McKay.

Bloom, B. (1984). The search for methods of group instruction as effective as one-to-one tutoring. *Educational Leadership, 41* (8), 4–17.

Bonne, R. (1985). *I know an old lady.* New York: Scholastic.

Bracey, G. (1987). The social impact of ability grouping. *Phi Delta Kappan, 68,* 701–702.

Bradley, K. B. (2001). *Pop! A book about bubbles.* New York: HarperTrophy.

Bransford, J. D., & McCarrell, N. S. (1974). A sketch of a cognitive approach to comprehension. In W. B. Weimer & D. S. Palermo (Eds.), *Cognition and the symbolic processes.* Hillsdale, NJ: Erlbaum.

Brinckloe, J. (1985). *Fireflies!* New York: Aladdin.

Bromley, K. (1996). *Webbing with literature: Creating story maps with children's books.* Boston: Allyn and Bacon.

Brown, A. (1975). Recognition, reconstruction, and recall of narrative sequences of preoperational children. *Child Development, 46,* 155–156.

Brown, D. (2007). *The train jumper.* New York: Roaring Brook.

Brown, R. (2008). The road not yet taken: A transactional strategies approach to comprehension instruction. *The Reading Teacher, 61,* 538–547.

Bruchac, J. (1993). *The first strawberries.* New York: Penguin Puffin.

Buehl, C. (2001). *Classroom strategies for interactive learning* (2nd ed.). Newark, DE: International Reading Association.

Bunting, E. (1995). *Train to somewhere.* New York: Clarion.

Burton, V. L. (1967). *Mike Mulligan and his steam shovel.* Boston: Houghton Mifflin.

Cannon, J. (1993). *Stellaluna.* San Diego, CA: Harcourt Brace.

Castek, J., Bevans-Mangelson, J. B., & Goldstone, B. (2006). Reading adventures online: Five ways to introduce the new literacies of the Internet through children's literature. *The Reading Teacher, 59,* 714–728.

Cauley, L. B. (1981). *Goldilocks and the three bears.* New York: Putnam.

Choi, Y. (2001). *The name jar.* New York: Knopf.

Choldenko, G. (2004). *Al Capone does my shirts.* New York: G. P. Putnam's Sons.

Chomsky, C. (1972). Stages in language development and reading exposure. *Harvard Educational Review, 42,* 1–33.

Christensen, L. (2000). *Reading, writing, and rising up: Teaching about social justice and the power of the word.* Milwaukee, WI: Rethinking Schools Ltd.

Cleary, B. (1975). *Ramona and her father.* New York: Dell.

Clements, A. (1998). *Frindle.* New York: Aladdin.

Clements, A. (2002). *Things not seen.* New York: Philomel.

Climo, S. (1989). *The Egyptian Cinderella.* New York: Thomas Y. Crowell.

Cobb, V. (2003). *I face the wind.* New York: HarperCollins

Cohen, D. (1968). The effect of literature on vocabulary and reading achievement. *Elementary English, 45,* 209–213, 217.

Colangelo, N., Assouline, S. G., & Gross, M. U. M. (2004). *A nation deceived: How schools hold back America's brightest students,* Volume 1. The Templeton National Report on Acceleration. University of Iowa: The Connie Belin & Jacqueline N. Blank International Center for Gifted Education and Talent Development. www.accelerationinstitute.org/Nation_Deceived/ND_v1.pdf.

Collier, J. L., & Collier, C. (1974). *My brother Sam is dead.* New York: Four Winds.

Craig, M. J. (1968). *The three wishes.* New York: Scholastic.

Creech, S. (1996). *Walk two moons.* New York: HarperTrophy.

Creech, S. (2001). *A fine, fine school.* New York: HarperCollins.

Creech. S. (2001). *Love that dog.* New York: HarperCollins.

Cummins, J. (1979). Linguistic interdependence and educational development in bilingual children. *Review of Educational Research, 49,* 222–251.

Cummins, J. (1994). Primary language instruction and the education of language minority students. In *Schooling and language minority students: A theoretical framework* (2nd ed., pp. 3–46). Sacramento: California State Department of Education.

Curtis, C. P. (1995). *The Watsons go to Birmingham—1963.* New York: Bantam Doubleday Dell.

Curtis, C. P. (2007). *Elijah of Buxton.* New York: Scholastic.

Cutts, D. (1979). *The house that Jack built:* Mahwah, NJ: Troll Associates.

Daniels, H. (1994). *Literature circles: Voice and choice in the student-centered classroom.* York, ME: Stenhouse.

Davies, N. (2003). *Surprising sharks.* Cambridge, MA: Candlewick.

de Angeli, M. (1949). *The door in the wall.* New York: Scholastic.

DeFord, D. (1981). Literacy: Reading, writing, and other essentials. *Language Arts, 58,* 652–658.

DeFord, D. (1984). Classroom contexts for literacy learning. In T. Raphael (Ed.), *The context of school-based literacy* (pp. 163–180). New York: Random House.

DeGroff, L., & Galda, L. (1992). Responding to literature: Activities for exploring books. In B. Cullinan (Ed.), *Invitation to read: More children's literature in the reading program.* Newark, DE: International Reading Association.

DiCamillo, K. (2000). *Because of Winn-Dixie.* Cambridge, MA: Candlewick.

DiCamillo, K. (2005). Character is the engine. In N. L. Roser & M. G. Martinez (Eds.), *What a character! Character study as a guide to literary meaning making in grades K–8* (pp. 26–35). Newark, DE: International Reading Association.

Dickson, S. V., Simmons, D. C., & Kame'enui, E. J. (1998). Text organization: Research bases. In D. C. Simmons & E. J. Kame'enui (Eds.), *What reading research tells us about children with diverse learning needs: Bases and basics* (pp. 239–277). Mahwah, NJ: Erlbaum.

Dole, J. A., Brown, K. J., & Trathen, W. (1996). The effects of strategy instruction on the comprehension performance of at-risk students. *Reading Research Quarterly, 31,* 62–88.

Dreher, M. J. (2003). Motivating teachers to read. *The Reading Teacher, 56,* 338–340.

Droop, M., & Verhoeven, L. (1998). Background knowledge, linguistic complexity, and second-language reading comprehension. *Journal of Literacy Research, 30,* 253–271.

Duke, N. (1999). *The scarcity of informational text in first grade.* University of Michigan-Ann Arbor: Center for the Improvement of Early Reading Achievement.

Duke, N. K., & Pearson, P. D. (2002). Effective practices for developing reading comprehension. In A. E. Farstrup & S. J. Samuels (Eds.), *What research has to say about reading instruction* (3rd ed., pp. 205–242). Newark, DE: International Reading Association.

Dunning, S., & Stafford, W. (1992). *Getting the knack: 20 poetry writing exercises.* Urbana, IL: National Council of Teachers of English.

Dunphy, M. (1999). *Here is the African savanna.* New York: Hyperion.

Dunphy, M. (2007). *Here is the Arctic winter.* Berkeley, CA: Web of Life.

Durkin, D. (1979). What classroom observations reveal about reading comprehension instruction. *Reading Research Quarterly, 14,* 481–533.

Dyson, A. H., & Freedman, S. W. (2003). Writing. In J. Flood, D. Lapp, J. R. Squire, & J M. Jensen (Eds.), *Handbook on research on teaching the English language arts* (2nd ed., pp. 967–992). Mahwah, NJ: Erlbaum.

Eckhoff, B. (1983). How reading affects children's writing. *Language Arts, 60,* 607–616.

Edelsky, C. (1988). Living in the author's world: Analyzing the author's craft. *The California Reader, 21,* 9–14.

Eeds, M., & Wells, D. (1989). Grand conversations: An explanation of meaning construction in literature study groups. *Research in the Teaching of English, 23,* 4–29.

Ehlert, L. (2001). *Waiting for wings.* San Diego: Harcourt.

Eldredge, J., & Butterfield, D. (1986). Alternatives to traditional reading instruction. *The Reading Teacher, 40,* 32–37.

Emery, D. (1996). Helping readers comprehend stories from the characters' perspectives. *The Reading Teacher, 49,* 534–541.

Emig, J. (1971). The *composing processes of twelfth graders* (Research Rep. No. 13). Urbana, IL: National Council of Teachers of English.

Ets, M. H. (1963). *Gilberto and the wind.* New York: Scholastic.

Farmer, J. (1999). *Bananas!* Watertown, MA: Charlesbridge.

Feitelson, D., Kita, B., & Goldstein, Z. (1986). Effects of listening to series stories on first graders' comprehension and use of language. *Research in the Teaching of English, 20,* 339–355.

Fisher, D., & Frey, N. (2003). Writing instruction for struggling adolescent readers: A gradual release model. *Journal of Adolescent and Adult Literacy, 46,* 396–405.

Fleischman, P. (1988). *Joyful noise.* New York: HarperTrophy.

Fleischman, S. (1963). *By the great horn spoon!* Boston: Little, Brown.

Fletcher, R. (1998). *Flying solo.* New York: Clarion.

Forbes, E. (1971). *Johnny Tremain.* New York: Dell.

Forehand, M. (2005). Bloom's taxonomy: Original and revised. In M. Orey (Ed.), *Emerging perspectives on learning, teaching, and technology.* Retrieved July 15, 2008, from http://projects.coe.uga.edu/epitt/.

Frost, R. (1959). *You come too.* New York: Holt, Rinehart and Winston.

Fuhler, C. (1994). Response journals: Just one more time with feeling. *Journal of Reading, 37,* 400–405.

Galda, L., & Cullinan, B. E. (2003). Literature for literacy: What research says about the benefits of using trade books in the classroom. In J. Flood, D. Lapp, J. R. Squire, & J. M. Jensen (Eds.), *Handbook of research on teaching the English language arts* (2nd ed., pp. 640–648). Mahwah, NJ: Erlbaum.

Gambrell, L. B. (2004). Shifts in the conversation: Teacher-led, peer-led, and computer-mediated discussions. *The Reading Teacher, 58,* 212–215.

Gannett, R. S. (1948). *My father's dragon.* New York: Random House.

Gantos, J. (2000). *Joey Pigza loses control.* New York: Farrar, Straus & Giroux.

George, J. C. (1972). *Julie of the wolves.* New York: Harper & Row.

Gibbons, G. (1993). *Frogs.* New York: Holiday House.

Gibbons, G. (1993). *From seed to plant.* New York: Holiday House.

Gibbons, G. (1995). *Sea turtles.* New York: Holiday House.

Gibbons, G. (1998). *Marshes & swamps.* New York: Holiday House.

Gibbons, G. (1998). *Yippee-yay!* New York: Little, Brown.

Glaser, L. (1992). *Wonderful worms.* Brookfield, CT: Millbrook.

Goldenberg, C. (1996). The education of language-minority students: Where are we, and where do we go from here? *The Elementary School Journal, 96,* 353–361.

Goldenberg, C. (2008, Summer). Teaching English Language Learners: What research does—and does not—say. *American Educator, 32,* 42–44.

Golenbock, P. (1990). *Teammates.* San Diego, CA: Harcourt Brace.

Graves, D. (1975). An examination of the writing processes of seven-year-old children. *Research in the Teaching of English, 9,* 227–241.

Graves, M. F., Juel, C., & Graves, B. B. (2004). *Teaching reading in the 21st century* (3rd ed.). Boston: Allyn and Bacon.

Gray, E. J. (1942). *Adam of the road.* New York: Puffin.

Grossman, P. (1999). *Very first things to know about frogs.* New York: Workman.

Gunning, T. (2008). *Creating literacy instruction for all students* (6th ed.). Boston: Allyn and Bacon.

Guthrie, J. T., & Ozgungor, S. (2002). Instructional contexts for reading engagement. In C. C. Block & M. Pressley (Eds.), *Comprehension instruction: Research-based best practices* (pp. 275–288). New York: Guilford.

Guthrie, J. T., & Wigfield, A. (2000). Engagement and motivation in reading. In M. L. Kamil, P. B. Mosenthal, P. D. Pearson, & R. Barr (Eds.), *Handbook of reading research, volume II* (pp. 403–422). Mahwah, NJ: Erlbaum.

Haddix, M. (1995). *Running out of time.* New York: Aladdin.

Hagerty, P., Hiebert, E., & Owens, M. (1989). Students' comprehension, writing, and perceptions in two approaches to literacy instruction. In S. McCormick & J. Zutell (Eds.), *Cognitive and social perspectives for literacy research and instruction* (pp. 453–459). Chicago: National Reading Conference.

Hancock, M. (1993). Character journals: Initiating involvement and identification through literature. *Journal of Reading, 37,* 42–50.

Harste, J. C., Short, K. G., & Burke, C. (1988). *Creating classrooms for authors.* Portsmouth: NH: Heinemann.

Hartman, D. K., & Hartman, J. A. (1993). Reading across texts: Expanding the role of the reader. *The Reading Teacher, 47,* 202–211.

Haskell, S. (1987). Literature mapping. *The California Reader, 20,* 29–31.

Hefflin, B. R., & Barksdale-Ladd, M. A. (2001). African American children's literature that helps students find themselves: Selection guidelines for grades K–3. *The Reading Teacher, 54,* 810–819.

Henkes, K. (1990). *Julius the baby of the world.* New York: Greenwillow.

Henkes, K. (1991). *Chrysanthemum.* New York: Greenwillow.

Henkes, K. (2003). *Olive's ocean.* New York: Greenwillow.

Henry, L. A. (2006). SEARCHing for an answer: The critical role of new literacies while reading on the Internet. *The Reading Teacher, 59,* 614–627.

Hesse, K. (1997). *Out of the dust.* New York: Scholastic.

Heuer, K. (2007). *Being caribou: Five months on foot with an Arctic herd.* New York: Walker & Co.

Hiaasen, C. (2002). *Hoot.* New York: Knopf.

Hill, K. (2000). *The year of Miss Agnes.* New York: Aladdin.

Hirsch, Jr., E. D. (2006). Building knowledge. *American Educator.* Retrieved July 14, 2008, from www.aft.org/pubs-reports/american_educator/issues/spring06/hirsch.htm.

Hoban, R. (1993). *Bread and jam for Frances.* New York: HarperCollins.

Hobbs, W. (1989). *Bearstone.* New York: Avon.

Hodges, M. (1964). *The wave.* Boston: Houghton Mifflin.

Hoffman, J. V. (1992). Critical reading/thinking across the curriculum. Using I-charts to support learning. *Language Arts, 69,* 121–127.

Hoffman, M. (1991). *Amazing Grace.* New York: Dial.

Hooks, W. (1987). *Moss gown.* New York: Clarion Books.

Horvath, P. (1991). *Everything on a waffle.* New York: Scholastic.

Howard, E. F. (2000). *Virgie goes to school with us boys.* New York: Simon & Schuster.

Ivers, K. S., & Barron, A. (2006). *Multimedia projects in education: Designing, producing, and assessing* (3rd ed.). Westport, CT: Libraries Unlimited.

Jenkins, S. (2007). *Living color.* Boston: Houghton Mifflin.

Johnson, T., & Louis, D. (1987). *Literacy through literature.* Portsmouth, NH: Heinemann.

Kadohata, C. (2004). *Kira-kira.* New York: Atheneum.

Keller, H. (1994). *Geraldine's baby brother.* New York: Morrow.

Kelly, P., & Farnan, N. (1991). Promoting critical thinking through response logs: A reader-response approach with fourth graders. In J. Zutell & S. McCormick (Eds.), *Learner factors/Teacher factors: Issues in literacy research and instruction.* Fortieth Yearbook of the National Reading Conference. Chicago: National Reading Conference.

Kennedy, K. (2003). Writing with Web logs. *Technology and Learning.* Retrieved July 4, 2008, from www.techlearning.com/db)area/archives/TL/2003/02/blogs/php.

Kiefer, B., Hepler, S., & Hickman, J. (2006). *Charlotte Huck's children's literature* (9th ed.). Columbus, OH: McGraw-Hill.

Konigsburg, E. L. (1974). *From the mixed-up files of Mrs. Basil E. Frankweiler.* New York: Dell.

Koskinen, P., Gambrell, L., Kapinus, B., & Heathington, B. (1988). Retelling: A strategy for enhancing students' reading comprehension. *The Reading Teacher, 41,* 892–896.

Krashen, S. (1982). *Principles and practices in second language acquisition.* Oxford: Pergamon.

Krashen, S. (2004). The case for narrow reading. *Language Magazine, 3* (5), 17–19.

Krathwohl, D. R. (2002). A revision of Bloom's Taxonomy: An overview. *Theory into Practice, 41,* 212–218.

Krull, K. (2003). *Harvesting hope: The story of Cesar Chavez.* San Diego, CA: Harcourt.

Kurlansky, M. (2006). *The story of salt.* New York: G. P. Putnam's Sons.

Lancia, P. J. (1997). Literary borrowing: The effects of literature on children's writing. *The Reading Teacher, 50,* 470–475.

Langer, J. (1995). *Envisioning literature: Literary understanding and literature instruction.* New York: Teacher College Press.

Langer, J., Applebee, A., Mullis, I., & Foertsch, M. (1990). *Learning to read in our nation's schools: Instruction and achievement in 1988 at grades 4, 8, and 12. National Assessment of Educational Progress.* Princeton, NJ: Educational Testing Service.

Langstaff, J. (1973). *Over in the meadow.* New York: Harcourt Brace Jovanovich.

Larrick, N. (1987). Illiteracy starts too soon. *Phi Delta Kappan, 69,* 184–189.

Lauber, P. (1998). *Painters of the caves.* New York: Scholastic.

Leaf, M. (1967). *The story of Ferdinand.* New York: Scholastic.

Lee, J., Grigg, W., & Donahue, P. (2007). *The nation's report card: Reading 2007* (NCES 2007-296). Washington, DC: National Center for Education Statistics, Institute of Education Sciences, U.S. Department of Education.

Leslie, L., & Allen, L. (1999). Factors that predict success in an early literacy intervention project. *Reading Research Quarterly, 34,* 404–424.

Leu, Jr., D. J., Castek, J., Henry, L. A., Coiro, J., & McMullan, M. (2004). The lessons that children teach us: Integrating children's literature and the new literacies of the Internet. *The Reading Teacher, 57,* 496–503.

Leu, Jr., D. J., Kinzer, C. K., Coiro, J. L., & Cammack, D. W. (2004). Toward a theory of new literacies emerging from the Internet and other information and communication technologies. In R. B. Ruddell & N. J. Unrau (Eds.), *Theoretical models and processes of reading* (5th ed., pp. 1570–1613). Newark, DE: International Reading Association.

Levinson, N.S. (2002). *North Pole South Pole.* New York: Holiday House.

Levitin, S. (1971). *Journey to America.* New York: Atheneum.

Li, G. (2004). Perspectives on struggling English language learners: Case studies of two Chinese-Canadian children. *Journal of Literacy Research, 36,* 31–72.

Lindop, L. (2003). *Probing volcanoes.* Fairfield, IA: 21st Century Books.

Littledale, F. (1986). *The magic fish.* New York: Scholastic.

London, J. (1974). *Call of the wild.* New York: Simon & Schuster.

Look, L. (2006). *Uncle Peter's amazing Chinese wedding.* New York: Atheneum.

Lord, B. (1984). *In the year of the boar and Jackie Robinson.* New York: Harper Junior Books.

Lord, C. (2006). *Rules.* New York: Scholastic.

Louie, A. L. (1982). *Yeh-Shen: A Cinderella story from China.* New York: Philomel.

Lowry, L. (1989). *Number the stars.* New York: Dell.

Lyon, G. E. (1999). *Where I'm from: Where poems come from.* Spring, TX: Absey.

Mandeville, T. F. (1994). KWLA: Linking the affective and cognitive domains. *The Reading Teacher, 47,* 679–680.

Manyak, P. (2007). Character trait vocabulary: A schoolwide approach. *The Reading Teacher, 69,* 574–577.

McKissack, P. (1986). *Flossie & the Fox.* New York: Dial.

McNeil, J. (1987). *Reading comprehension: New directions for classroom practice* (2nd ed.). Glenview, IL: Scott, Foresman.

Meier, T. (2003). "Why can't she remember that?" The importance of storybook reading in multilingual, multicultural classrooms. *The Reading Teacher, 57,* 242–252.

Michelson, R. (2006). *Across the alley.* New York: G. P. Putnam's Sons.

Morgan, R., & Albritton, J. D. (1990). Primary students respond to literature through partner journals. *The California Reader, 23,* 29–30.

Morrow, L. M. (1985). Retelling stories: A strategy for improving young children's comprehension, concept of story structure, and oral language complexity. *The Elementary School Journal, 85,* 647–661.

Morrow, L. M. (1992). The impact of a literature-based program on literacy achievement, use of literature, and attitudes of children from minority backgrounds. *Reading Research Quarterly, 27,* 250–275.

Morrow, L. M. (2003). Motivating lifelong voluntary readers. In J. Flood, D. Lapp, J. R. Squire, & J. M. Jensen (Eds.), *Handbook of research on teaching the English language arts* (2nd ed., pp. 857–867). Mahwah, NJ: Erlbaum.

Morrow, L. M., & Gambrell, L. B. (2000). Literature-based reading instruction. In M. L. Kamil, P. B. Mosenthal, P. D. Pearson, & R. Barr (Eds.), *Handbook of reading research, volume II* (pp. 563–586). Mahwah, NJ: Erlbaum.

Morrow, L. M., O'Connor, E., & Smith, J. (1990). Effects of a story reading program on the literacy development of at risk kindergarten children. *Journal of Reading Behavior, 22,* 255–275.

Munsch, R. (1980). *The paper bag princess.* Toronto, Ontario: Annick.

Murphy, J. (2003). *An American plague: The true and terrifying story of the yellow fever epidemic of 1793.* New York: Clarion.

Nagy, W., Herman, P., & Anderson, R. (1985). Learning words from context. *Reading Research Quarterly, 20,* 233–253.

National Association for Gifted Children. (2008). *The NAGC standards: Curriculum and instruction.* Retrieved July 20, 2008, from www.nagc.org/index.aspx?id=544.

National Reading Panel. (2000). *Teaching children to read: An evidence-based assessment of scientific research literature on reading and its implications for reading instruction* (NIH Publication No. 00-4769). Washington, DC: U.S. Government Printing Office.

NCELA. (2006). *How many school-aged English language learners (ELLs) are there in the U.S.?* Washington, DC: National Clearinghouse for English Language Acquisition and Language Instruction Educational Programs. Retrieved May 20, 2008, from www.ncela.gwu.edu/expert/faq/01leps.html.

Nelson, V. M. (2003). *Almost to freedom.* Minneapolis: Carolrhoda.

Nixon, J. L. (1987). *A family apart.* Toronto: Bantam.

Noble, T. H. (2007). *The orange shoes.* Chelsea, MI: Sleeping Bear Press.

Nokes, J. D. (2008). The Observation/Inference Chart: Improving students' abilities to make inferences while reading nontraditional texts. *Journal of Adolescent and Adult Literacy, 51,* 538–546.

Nolte, R. Y., & Singer, H. (1985). Active comprehension: Teaching a process of reading comprehension and its effects on reading achievement. *The Reading Teacher, 39,* 24–31.

O'Dell, S. (1960). *Island of the Blue Dolphins.* Boston: Houghton Mifflin.

Ogle, D. (1986). K-W-L: A teaching model that develops active reading of expository text. *The Reading Teacher, 39,* 564–570.

Palmer, B. M., Codling, R. M., & Gambrell, L. B. (1994). In their own words: What elementary students have to say about motivation to read. *The Reading Teacher, 48,* 176–178.

Park, L. S. (2002). *When my name was Keoko.* New York: Dell Yearling.

Park, L. S. (2001). *A single shard.* New York: Clarion.

Parker, N. W. (1995). *Money, money, money.* New York: HarperCollins.

Parker, S. (1999). *It's a frog's life.* Pleasantville, NY: Reader's Digest Children's Books.

Paulsen, G. (1987). *Hatchet.* New York: The Trumpet Club.

Peet, B. (1970). *The whingdingdilly.* Boston: Houghton Mifflin.

Peregoy, S. F., & Boyle, O. F. (2009). *Reading, writing, and learning in ESL.* Boston: Pearson.

Perkins, L. R. (2005). *Criss cross.* New York: Harper Trophy.

Petty, K. (1998). *I didn't know that crocodiles yawn to keep cool.* Brookfield, CT: Copper Beech.

Polacco, P. (1990). *Thunder cake.* New York: Philomel.

Potter, B. (1989). *The tale of Peter Rabbit.* London: Penguin.

Pressley, M. (2002). Comprehension strategies instruction: A turn-of-the-century status report. In C. C. Block & M. Pressley (Eds.), *Comprehension instruction: Research-based best practices* (pp. 11–27). New York: Guilford.

Purcell-Gates, V., McIntyre, E., & Freppon, P. A. (1995). Learning written storybook language in school: A comparison of low-SES children in skills-based and whole-language classroom. *American Educational Research Journal, 32,* 659–685.

RAND Reading Study Group. (2002). *Reading for understanding: Toward an R & D program in reading comprehension.* Santa Monica, CA: RAND.

Raphael, T. (2000). Balancing literature and instruction: Lessons from the Book Club Project. In B. Taylor, M. Graves, & P. van den Broek (Eds.), *Reading for meaning: Fostering comprehension in the middle grades* (pp. 70–94). New York: Teachers College Press.

Rathman, P. (1995). *Officer Buckle and Gloria.* New York: Scholastic.

Rawls, W. (1961). *Where the red fern grows.* New York: Doubleday.

Readence, J., Bean, T., & Baldwin, R. (1981). *Content area reading: An integrated approach.* Dubuque, IA: Kendall/Hunt.

Reasoner, C. F. (1976). *Releasing children to literature* (rev. ed.). New York: Dell.

Recorvits, H. (2003). *My name is Yoon.* New York: Frances Foster.

Reutzel, D. R., Smith, J. A., & Fawson, P. D. (2005). An evaluation of two approaches for teaching reading comprehension strategies in the primary years using science information texts. *Early Childhood Research Quarterly, 20,* 276–305.

Richards, I. A. (1929). *Practical criticism: A study of literary judgment.* New York: Harcourt.

Rockwell, A. (2000). *Only passing through: The story of Sojourner Truth.* New York: Dell Dragonfly.

Roehler, L., & Duffy, G. G. (1984). Direct explanation of comprehension processes. In G. G. Duffy, L. R. Roehler, & J. Mason (Eds.), *Comprehension instruction: Perspectives and suggestions* (pp. 265–280). New York: Longman.

Romanek, T. (2002). *Zzz . . . The most interesting book you'll ever read about sleep.* Toronto: Kids Can Press.

Romano, T. (2000). *Blending genre, altering style.* Portsmouth, NH: Boynton/Cook.

Rosenblatt, L. M. (1938). *Literature as exploration.* New York: Appleton-Century.

Roser, N. L., & Martinez, M. G. (Eds.) (2005). *What a character! Character study as a guide to literary meaning making in grades K–8.* Newark, DE: International Reading Association.

Roth, S. L. (2001). *Happy birthday Mr. Kang.* Washington, DC: National Geographic.

Ryan, P. M. (2000). *Esperanza rising.* New York: Scholastic.

Saul, E. W. (Ed.). (2004). *Crossing borders in literacy and science instruction.* Newark, DE: International Reading Association.

Say, A. (1993). *Grandfather's journey.* New York: Houghton Mifflin.

Schlitz, L. A. (2007). *Good masters! Sweet ladies!* Cambridge, MA: Candlewick.

Schmidt, G. (2007). *The Wednesday wars.* New York: Clarion.

Schmitt, N., & Carter, R. (2000). The lexical advantages of narrow reading for second language learners. *TESOL Journal, 9* (1), 4–9.

Schyffert, B. U. (2003 translation). *The man who went to the far side of the moon.* San Francisco: Chronicle.

Selznick, B. (2007). *The invention of Hugo Cabret.* New York: Scholastic.

Seuling, B. (2003). *Flick a switch: How electricity gets to your home.* New York: Holiday House.

Shanahan, T. (1988). The reading-writing relationship: Seven instructional principles. *The Reading Teacher, 41,* 756–761.

Shanahan, T., & Shanahan, S. (1997). Character perspective charting: Helping children to develop a more complete conception of story. *The Reading Teacher, 50,* 668–677.

Short, K. G., Kauffman, G., & Kahn, L. H. (2000). "I just need to draw": Responding to literature across multiple sign systems. *The Reading Teacher, 54,* 160–171.

Simon, S. (2003). *The moon.* New York: Simon & Schuster.

Simon, S. (2006). *Horses.* New York: HarperCollins.

Sinatra, R., Stahl-Gemake, J., & Berg, D. (1984). Improving reading comprehension of disabled readers through semantic mapping. *The Reading Teacher, 38,* 22–29.

Sorensen, V. (1957). *Miracles on Maple Hill.* New York: Harcourt Brace & World.

Southgate, V. (1966). *The little red hen.* Loughborough, England: Wills & Hepworth.

Speare, E. G. (1983). *The sign of the beaver.* Boston: Houghton Mifflin.

Spinelli, J. (2002). *Stargirl.* New York: Knopf.

Stahl, S., & Vancil, S. (1986). Discussion is what makes semantic maps work in vocabulary instruction. *The Reading Teacher, 40,* 62–67.

Starosta, P. (1996). *The frog.* Watertown, MA: Charlesbridge.

Steig, W. (1969). *Sylvester and the magic pebble.* New York: Simon & Schuster.

Steig, W. (1982). *Doctor DeSoto.* New York: Farrar, Straus & Giroux.

Taba, H. (1967). *Teachers' handbook for elementary social studies.* Reading, MA: Addison-Wesley.

Taylor, B. M., Pearson, P. D., Clark, K. F., & Walpole, S. (1999). *Beating the odds in teaching all children to read.* University of Michigan–Ann Arbor: Center for the Improvement of Early Reading Achievement.

Taylor, M. (1983). *Roll of thunder, hear my cry.* Toronto: Bantam.

Thayer, E. L. (1952). Casey at the bat. In David L. George (Ed.), *The family book of best loved poems* (pp. 411–412). Garden City, NY: Hanover House.

Tomlinson, C. A. (2001). *How to differentiate instruction in mixed-ability classrooms* (2nd ed.). Alexandria, VA: Association for Supervision and Curriculum Development.

Tomlinson, C. A., Brighton, C., Hertberg, H., Callahan, C. M., Moon, T. R., Brimijoin, K., Conover, L. A., & Reyholds, T. (2003). Differentiating instruction in response to student readiness, interest, and learning profile in academically diverse classrooms: A review of literature. *Journal for the Education of the Gifted, 27,* 119–145.

Tunnell, M., & Jacobs, J. (1989). Using "real" books: Research findings on literature based reading instruction. *The Reading Teacher, 42,* 470–477.

U'Ren, A. (2003). *Mary Smith.* New York: Farrar, Straus & Giroux.

Uchida, Y. (1971). *Journey to Topaz.* New York: Charles Scribner's Sons.

Vaughn, S. R., Bos, C. S., & Schumm, J. S. (2007). *Teaching students who are exceptional, diverse, and at risk in the general education classroom* (4th ed.). Boston: Allyn and Bacon.

Viorst, J. (1972). *Alexander and the terrible, horrible, no good, very bad day.* New York: Atheneum.

Vygotsky, L. (1978). *Mind in society.* Cambridge, MA: Harvard University Press.

Waber, B. (1975). *Ira sleeps over.* Boston: Houghton Mifflin.

Walmsley, S., & Walp, T. (1989). *Teaching literature in elementary school.* Albany: Center for the Learning and Teaching of Literature, University at Albany, State University of New York.

Wendler, D., Samuels, S. J., & Moore, V. (1989). The comprehension instruction of award-winning teachers, teachers with master's degrees, and other teachers. *Reading Research Quarterly, 24,* 382–401.

Western, L. (1980). A comparative study of literature through folk tale variants. *Language Arts, 57,* 395–402.

Wexler, J. (1987). *Flowers fruits seeds.* New York: Simon & Schuster.

White, E. B. (1952). *Charlotte's web.* New York: Harper & Row.

White, E. B. (1973). *Stuart Little.* New York: Harper & Row.

Whitin, P. (2002). Leading into literature circles through the sketch-to-stretch strategy. *The Reading Teacher, 55,* 444–454.

Wick, W. (1997). *A drop of water.* New York: Scholastic.

Wiencek, J., & O'Flahavan, J. (1994). From teacher-led to peer discussions about literature: Suggestions for making the shift. *Language Arts, 71,* 448–498.

Wilhelm, J. (2007). *Engaging readers & writers with inquiry.* New York: Scholastic.

Wilhelm, J. D. (2002). *Action strategies for deepening comprehension.* New York: Scholastic.

Willingham, D. T. (2006, Spring). How knowledge helps. *American Educator,* 30–37.

Willingham, D. T. (2006–07, Winter). The usefulness of *brief* instruction in reading comprehension strategies. *American Educator,* 39–45, 50.

Wolf, M. (2007). *Proust and the squid: The story and science of the reading brain.* New York: HarperCollins.

Woods, B. (2002). *The red rose box.* New York: Puffin.

Woodson, J. (2003). *Locomotion.* New York: Grosset & Dunlap.

Worthy, J. (2000). Teachers' and students' suggestions for motivating middle-school students to read. In T. Shanahan & F. V. Rodriguez-Brown (Eds.), *National Reading Conference yearbook, 49* (pp. 441–451). Chicago: National Reading Conference.

Worthy, J. (2002). What makes intermediate-grade students want to read? *The Reading Teacher, 55,* 568–569.

Wuthrick, M. (1990). Blue jays win! Crows go down in defeat! *Phi Delta Kappan, 71,* 553–556.

Yenawine, P. (1997). Thoughts on visual literacy. In J. Flood, S. B. Heath, and D. Lapp (Eds.), *Handbook of research on teaching literacy through the communicative and visual arts* (pp. 845–846). New York: Macmillan.

Yep, L. (1975). *Dragonwings.* New York: Harper Junior Books.

Yep, L. (1993). *Dragon's gate.* New York: HarperCollins.

Yep, L. (1995). *Dragon's gate.* New York: HarperTrophy.

Yopp, H. K., & Yopp, R. H. (2003). Ten important words: Identifying the big ideas in informational text. *Journal of Content Area Reading, 2,* 7–13.

Yopp, R. H. (1988). Questioning and active comprehension. *Questioning Exchange, 2,* 231–238.

Yopp, R. H., & Yopp, H. K. (2003). Time with text. *The Reading Teacher, 57,* 284–287.

Yopp, R. H., & Yopp, H. K. (2004). Preview-predict-confirm: Thinking about the language and content of informational text. *The Reading Teacher, 58,* 79–83.

Yopp, R. H., & Yopp, H. K. (2006). Informational texts as read-alouds at home and school. *Journal of Literacy Research, 38*(1), 37–51.

# Index